"To persist in overcomi[...] the Story (Revelation 1[...] this book share powerfu[...] of a host of influential f[...] but not limited to Harri[...] une, Fannie Lou Hamer, [...], John Lewis, Jackie Robinson, and the late Kobe Bryant. The contributors also discuss how God has used lesser-known figures, who have often escaped the purview of historians, such as Pastor Davidson, Brother Justice, and Dr. Frederick Sampson Jr. The devotions facilitate daily and deep meditation on the story of God in Scripture and the Black experience."

—Rev. Dr. Jonathan Chism, assistant professor of history, University of Houston-Downtown

"Integrating the richness of Scripture with the historical struggles and accomplishments of Black people, *Tell the Story: 40 Devotions with Reflections on Black History* will inform readers young and old of God's unfolding salvation drama in the lives of African Americans. This devotional is sure to teach, inspire, and embolden, engendering much-needed hope. In producing this devotional, Our Daily Bread Ministries has served well those of us who draw upon the rich spirituality of the Black Church and beyond. Its nuggets of reflection can be read again and again, making this devotional timeless."

—Raynard Smith, PhD, associate professor of pastoral care and pastoral theology, New Brunswick Theological Seminary

"These are the voices from whom I want to learn faith. Many have already been my teachers, and now they are sharing this beautiful gift with the church that God loves. If you're hungry to discover the fullness of how Jesus-the-Liberator has transformed the world, and continues to do it through His people, this book is for you. As you rediscover history through these fresh eyes, and hear from these important voices, the gospel of Jesus that is good news for the world will seem even bigger. You are going to meet God in these pages."

—Margot Starbuck, author and speaker

"As a Christian and a Southern girl who attended an HBCU and was active in the civil rights marches in the '60s, I could personally relate to many of the stories written here. More importantly, as a Southern girl, I love peach cobbler. As I read these 40 devotions that "tell the story," this experience reminded me of the joy I get when I devour a great peach cobbler. First is the top crust which is the Scripture, a foretaste of what is to come. Then the peaches comprise the filling just as the stories provide the sweet historical content either about a pivotal event in Black history or about a Black person who challenged the system to provide a great and lasting impact on society. At the bottom of all that sweetness is the bottom crust, the best part, which are the passages of Scripture that provide a deeper and relevant Word from the Lord. These 40 devotions are beautifully written and can be read at any time, but especially during Black History Month. It is a great way to learn about history and how that history relates to our lives, as well as a way to spend time with the Lord."

—Deacon Patricia Wallace, president,
Alfred Street Baptist Church Foundation

TELL THE STORY

40 Devotions with Reflections on Black History

Joyce Dinkins, General Editor

Our Daily Bread
Publishing™

Tell the Story: 40 Devotions with Reflections on Black History
© 2023 by Our Daily Bread Ministries

Entries by Stacy Hawkins Adams, Santes Beatty, Rasool Berry, Nia Caldwell, Anthony Cobbs, Joyce Dinkins, Marlena Graves, Georgia Hill, Noel Hutchinson, Arthur Jackson, Melanie Johnson, Kayla Jones, Chelsea Moore Jordan, Carey H. Latimore IV, Kimya Loder, Tondra L. Loder-Jackson, Michelle R. Loyd-Paige, Victoria Saunders McAfee, Marvin A. McMickle, Karynthia Phillips, Patricia Raybon, CJ Rhodes, Lisa D. Robinson, Cherie Trahan, Ekemini Uwan, Barbranda Lumpkins Walls, Linda Washington, B. Williams Waters, Marvin Williams, Roslyn Yilpet © Our Daily Bread Ministries. Used by permission.

Requests for permission to quote from this book should be directed to: Permissions Department, Our Daily Bread Publishing, PO Box 3566, Grand Rapids, MI 49501, or contact us by email at permissionsdept@odb.org.

For Scripture permissions, see page 195.

ISBN: 978-1-64070-223-3

Library of Congress Cataloging-in-Publication Data Available

Printed in the United States of America
23 24 25 26 27 28 29 30 / 8 7 6 5 4 3 2 1

To Carter G. Woodson, founder of the Association for the Study of African American Life and History, whose celebration of the lives of Black Americans led to the establishment of Black History Month

CONTENTS

CONTENTS | 9

INTRODUCTION
Our Stories, Our Faith

*For it is by grace you have been saved,
through faith—and this is not from
yourselves, it is the gift of God—not by
works, so that no one can boast. For
we are God's handiwork, created in
Christ Jesus to do good works, which
God prepared in advance for us to do.*

Ephesians 2:8–10

Here are forty brief devotionals that combine Bible reading with highlights from the lives of Black historymakers and events in the African American experience—encouraging and enlightening stories of God's grace and our faith. Alongside, eight feature articles reveal the beginnings of historically Black colleges and universities, Black denominations and churches, music genres, prayer practices, and more, helping readers see more deeply into the faith story of African Americans.

Consider the experiences of Amelia Boynton Robinson, John Lewis, Nannie Helen Burroughs, Benjamin Elijah Mays, Mary Smith Peake, James Cone, and dozens more, whose stories testify to God's powerful hand in our lives. This history affords opportunities for us to learn, celebrate, be encouraged, share, as well as to persevere. With faith in God, each of us can stand, too, whatever we may face, and we can dream.

Seeing God's hand in previous generations' history is an opportunity to learn and to teach others the overarching story of God's powerful love. Use these devotionals in your personal time and with your family and friends. Share with others on Martin Luther King Jr. Day, during Black History Month, on Juneteenth, Mother's Day, Father's Day, graduation day, and any day. In person, in a post, or in a presentation.

As you read these reflections, we believe you will be in awe of God and gain inspiration for your own story. That you will meditate on God's guidance in the Scriptures and yourself become "living proof" of the power of this faith that inspires, overcomes, protects, and causes people to thrive. We sincerely pray that *Tell the Story* encourages you to pursue a faith legacy of your own that becomes part of God's great story.

Joyce Dinkins
General Editor

TELL THE STORY

MIDDLE PASSAGE MILLIONS

Kayla Jones

*The Spirit of the Lord is on me,
because he has anointed me to
proclaim good news to the poor. He
has sent me to proclaim freedom for
the prisoners and recovery of sight for
the blind, to set the oppressed free.*

Luke 4:18

During my senior year of college, I participated
in a service-learning trip to Ghana, West Africa.
I visited and toured the Cape Coast Castle, one of
the key forts the transatlantic slave trade facilitated
for kidnapping, selling, and otherwise oppressing
many millions of Africans. Countless people per-
ished. One exhibit, Portraits of the Middle Passage,
showcased sculptures reimagining slavery's victims.
I looked at my Black people's traumatized faces and
felt sick about the pain experienced within those
prisons, aboard ships, and in foreigners' hands. But
I also know the enslaved dared to imagine a better

future for their descendants, resisted oppression, and pursued freedom. My freedom.

Jesus Christ denounced corrupt religious, economic, and sociopolitical systems, like chattel slavery—proclaiming the good news. Jesus pursued all people's freedom in this world, and He sacrificed His life so that we can be set free spiritually—eternally. Jesus declared God's demands for justice, love, and righteousness as He repeated Isaiah's prophecy (Luke 4:14–19; see Isaiah 61:1–2). Standing in the synagogue at Nazareth at the beginning of His ministry, Jesus determined to "set the oppressed free" (Luke 4:18).

The gospel calls us to imagine and to press for freedom with both strong teaching and sacrificial acts of love. We love our God and our neighbor fully when we raise our voices, too, against oppression and proclaim God's favor on all people. God has carried and will carry us through.

How does Jesus's mission to release captives, give sight to the blind, and liberate the oppressed change our perspective of the gospel and the hope He brings?

Heavenly Father, I praise You for the faith, imagination, and resiliency of my ancestors. Thank You for being my God of hope.

Luke 4:14–19

¹⁴Jesus returned to Galilee in the power of the Spirit, and news about him spread through the whole countryside. ¹⁵He was teaching in their synagogues, and everyone praised him.

¹⁶He went to Nazareth, where he had been brought up, and on the Sabbath day he went into the synagogue, as was his custom. He stood up to read, ¹⁷and the scroll of the prophet Isaiah was handed to him. Unrolling it, he found the place where it is written:

> ¹⁸"The Spirit of the Lord is on
> me,
>   because he has anointed me
>   to proclaim good news to
>   the poor.
> He has sent me to proclaim
>   freedom for the prisoners
>   and recovery of sight for the
>   blind,
> to set the oppressed free,
>   ¹⁹to proclaim the year of the
>   Lord's favor."

CELEBRATE FREEDOM

Victoria Saunders McAfee

Those who go out weeping, carrying seed to sow, will return with songs of joy, carrying sheaves with them.

Psalm 126:6

At eighty-nine years old, Opal Lee passionately pursued the goal of making Juneteenth a national holiday. Opal wanted the nation to celebrate June 19, 1865, when Union General Gordon Granger announced freedom to those still enslaved in Texas. Though the Union proclaimed emancipation in 1863, hundreds of thousands of slaves remained captive. Final Civil War skirmishes occurred into 1865, and many slaveholders escaped to Texas, where Confederates resisted, to keep their slaves. Ms. Lee spoke around the nation, and gained signatures on petitions to secure annual celebration of the day when the Union Army ordered emancipation of those who had remained in bondage. After five years of petitioning, on June 17, 2021, Opal Lee stood at the table as President Biden signed and declared Juneteenth a national holiday, commemorating African Americans' freedom from captivity.

Scripture commemorates when the Jewish exiles returned from captivity in Babylon, ascending to Jerusalem "with songs of joy," proclaiming God's faithfulness in their deliverance (Psalm 126:6). When the slaves in Texas learned they were no longer captives, they likewise remembered their sorrows and rejoiced in their liberation, praising God.

Continued Juneteenth observances remind us of hard-fought battles, and the freedom God declares. Scripture announces to all people of all generations that God sent Jesus "to proclaim freedom for the captives and release from darkness for the prisoners" (Isaiah 61:1). The more we understand our freedom through Christ, the more we can praise God for delivering us.

> Our declaration of freedom through
> Christ is a daily celebration.

*Lord, remind me and help me to celebrate
our spiritual freedom each day.*

Psalm 126

> ¹When the LORD restored the
> fortunes of Zion,

we were like those who
dreamed.
²Our mouths were filled with
laughter,
our tongues with songs of
joy.
Then it was said among the
nations,
"The LORD has done great
things for them."
³The LORD has done great
things for us,
and we are filled with joy.

⁴Restore our fortunes, LORD,
like streams in the Negev.
⁵Those who sow with tears
will reap with songs of joy.
⁶Those who go out weeping,
carrying seed to sow,
will return with songs of joy,
carrying sheaves with them.

ROOTED IN GOD

Linda Washington

*Let your roots grow down into him,
and let your lives be built on him.*

Colossians 2:7 NLT

God had a divine plan for Lott Carey, though he entered the world in 1780 as a slave in Virginia. Carey's grandmother Mihala told her grandson the truth about Jesus. And then she prayed, believing God would someday send Lott to Africa to tell people about the Lord. In 1807, God fully revealed His answer to Grandmother Mihala's prayers. Not long after hearing a certain sermon at First Baptist Church, Richmond, Virginia, Lott believed in Jesus as his Savior. Lott Carey did become the first African American Baptist missionary to Africa, in Liberia.

The apostle Paul writes of another grandmother, Lois, who shared the truth about Christ with her grandson Timothy from his childhood (2 Timothy 1:5). We read in Colossians that when Paul learned some believers at Colossae had heard false teachings about God, he wrote this letter with Timothy as co-sender, to remind those Colossian believers of the starting point of their faith—"Jesus as Lord" (Colossians 2:6).

Reminding the believers of that beginning, he wrote, "Continue to live your lives in him, rooted and built up in him, strengthened in the faith as you were taught, and overflowing with thankfulness" (2:6–7). By being deeply rooted in the truth of God, the believers wouldn't fall for the lies others spoke about God. If our roots are deep in the truth of God's Word, we won't fall for lies or be knocked over by the winds of change.

> Understanding Bible truths and reflecting on true stories of faith nurture and strengthen our lives.

God, thank You for Your divine plans for me, despite obstacles I face or untruths others speak. In Jesus's name, amen.

Colossians 2:1–7 NLT

¹I want you to know how much I have agonized for you and for the church at Laodicea, and for many other believers who have never met me personally. ²I want them to be encouraged and knit together by strong ties of love. I want them to have complete confidence that they understand

God's mysterious plan, which is Christ himself. ³In him lie hidden all the treasures of wisdom and knowledge.

⁴I am telling you this so no one will deceive you with well-crafted arguments. ⁵For though I am far away from you, my heart is with you. And I rejoice that you are living as you should and that your faith in Christ is strong.

⁶And now, just as you accepted Christ Jesus as your Lord, you must continue to follow him. ⁷Let your roots grow down into him, and let your lives be built on him. Then your faith will grow strong in the truth you were taught, and you will overflow with thankfulness.

COMMUNITY ENCOURAGEMENT

Chelsea Moore Jordan

*For even Christ didn't live
to please himself.*

Romans 15:3 NLT

The familiar sound of chatter filled the basement. This kind of fellowship—eating food and having conversations, sitting around casually together while also learning—filled my Sunday nights with the ones I call family. Eventually, our conversations would shift into sharing at a deeper level the joys and struggles of our lives, including in our marriages, families, and other relationships. We would partner wise direction with affirmations for each individual. At the end of the night, we could leave with encouragement and guidance on how to grow spiritually.

True community enables trust and vulnerability. As Paul encouraged those in the growing body of believers, Christians are uniquely called to "really love [others]" (Romans 12:9 NLT).

Benjamin Elijah Mays is a classic example of a

person who cultivated the kind of community that Paul described, one where believers have "the same attitude of mind toward each other that Christ Jesus had" (Romans 15:5). This mentor and Morehouse professor's influence spread across decades of leaders, most notably Dr. Martin Luther King Jr. Mays encouraged many to love in community.

We build each other up by loving one another, fellowshipping with and sharpening each other (Acts 2:42; Proverbs 27:17). When we follow Jesus's example of walking with others and pouring into them, we build a community that points to Him.

God values our communities.

God, thank You for helping me to find ways to reflect Your spirit as I walk with other Christian believers in community. I'm grateful. In Jesus's name, amen.

Romans 15:2–9 NLT

²We should help others do what is right and build them up in the Lord. ³For even Christ didn't live to please himself. As the Scriptures say, "The insults of those who insult you, O God, have fallen on me." ⁴Such things were written in the Scriptures long ago to teach us. And the Scriptures

give us hope and encouragement as we wait patiently for God's promises to be fulfilled.

⁵May God, who gives this patience and encouragement, help you live in complete harmony with each other, as is fitting for followers of Christ Jesus. ⁶Then all of you can join together with one voice, giving praise and glory to God, the Father of our Lord Jesus Christ.

⁷Therefore, accept each other just as Christ has accepted you so that God will be given glory. ⁸Remember that Christ came as a servant to the Jews to show that God is true to the promises he made to their ancestors. ⁹He also came so that the Gentiles might give glory to God for his mercies to them.

GO WITHOUT DOUBT

Patricia Raybon

What are you doing here, Elijah?
1 Kings 19:13

Some people laughed behind her back. Her down-home speech and country ways made her seem to some the least likely person to inspire and help lead a Freedom Summer movement that changed a nation in 1964. But the civil rights folk hero held audiences rapt with the one thing that mattered to her most—her undoubting answer to God's calling: *I will go.*

Thus, Fannie Lou Hamer went. Where? To register to vote, along with some seventeen thousand others—even though it cost them and only one thousand six hundred registrations were accepted. To jail, in the face of attacks and the murders of fellow civil rights volunteers. To end-of-the-road shacks, carrying the message of voter freedom to poor Blacks and Whites, her passion drawing gunfire by night riders.

Hamer said, "I guess if I'd had any sense, I'd

have been a little scared—but what was the point of being scared? The only thing they could do was kill me, and it kinda seemed like they'd been trying to do that a little bit at a time since I could remember."

Her brave clarity models the answer the Lord invites of us when He asks—as He inquired of His prophet Elijah—"What are you doing here?" (1 Kings 19:13). It's a question for all seeking to serve God. What are you doing *here*? Is this your rightful ministry or work?

> May we hear Him, as our heroes
> did, and answer without doubt.

When You ask for my service, Lord, may I clearly
hear Your calling, then go without doubt.

1 Kings 19:7–18

> ⁷The angel of the LORD came back a second
> time and touched him and said, "Get up
> and eat, for the journey is too much for
> you." ⁸So he got up and ate and drank.
> Strengthened by that food, he traveled
> forty days and forty nights until he reached
> Horeb, the mountain of God. ⁹There he
> went into a cave and spent the night.

TELL THE STORY

And the word of the LORD came to him: "What are you doing here, Elijah?"

¹⁰He replied, "I have been very zealous for the LORD God Almighty. The Israelites have rejected your covenant, torn down your altars, and put your prophets to death with the sword. I am the only one left, and now they are trying to kill me too."

¹¹The LORD said, "Go out and stand on the mountain in the presence of the LORD, for the LORD is about to pass by."

Then a great and powerful wind tore the mountains apart and shattered the rocks before the LORD, but the LORD was not in the wind. After the wind there was an earthquake, but the LORD was not in the earthquake. ¹²After the earthquake came a fire, but the LORD was not in the fire. And after the fire came a gentle whisper. ¹³When Elijah heard it, he pulled his cloak over his face and went out and stood at the mouth of the cave.

Then a voice said to him, "What are you doing here, Elijah?"

¹⁴He replied, "I have been very zealous for the LORD God Almighty. The Israelites have rejected your covenant, torn down your altars, and put your prophets to death

with the sword. I am the only one left, and now they are trying to kill me too."

¹⁵The Lord said to him, "Go back the way you came, and go to the Desert of Damascus. When you get there, anoint Hazael king over Aram. ¹⁶Also, anoint Jehu son of Nimshi king over Israel, and anoint Elisha son of Shaphat from Abel Meholah to succeed you as prophet. ¹⁷Jehu will put to death any who escape the sword of Hazael, and Elisha will put to death any who escape the sword of Jehu. ¹⁸Yet I reserve seven thousand in Israel—all whose knees have not bowed down to Baal and whose mouths have not kissed him."

AMAZING GRACE

Arthur Jackson

'Tis grace that brought me safe thus far, and grace will lead me home.

"Amazing Grace"

Many of us have had the experience of joining church on a Sunday morning and being greeted by the harmonies and melodies of music and voices that engage us in worship, ready our hearts for the Word, and help us face a week that looms large with unknown challenges. Among the beloved songs of the church that the Lord uses to strengthen souls, a song that has resonated among African American congregations, too, is "Amazing Grace." Aware of where the Lord has brought us from, conscious of rescue from a world that was ruining us, we personally identify with the first verse of the song:

> Amazing grace! how sweet the sound that saved a wretch like me! I once was lost, but now am found; was blind but now I see.

Reminders about God's grace—God's favor freely given to us through Christ—never grow old; and neither do the truths expressed in the other verses of the song, especially verse three.

> Through many dangers, toils and snares, I have already come; 'Tis grace that brought me safe thus far, and grace will lead me home.

Indeed, "life under the sun" has included unpleasant realities and "seasons of distress and grief." The pangs of poverty, the pain of disease, the discomfort of severed relationships, and other struggles have plagued us as individuals. And "dangers, toils and snares" have been and, in various ways, continue to be the lot of those who identify as African American. Our forebears were shackled and marked as the "property" of others. Physical restraints have disappeared but, along the way, various other restraints have come and gone. Even today, there are reminders that African American people are often not yet out of harm's way.

Israel, the ancient people of God, knew about dangers, toils, and snares. Horrible oppression came in the form of unreasonable, hard labor and genocide. Pain, ugliness, and messiness were real in the lives of God's people in Egypt. However, these things had not gone unnoticed. God was at work preparing an instrument of deliverance and listening to the groans of His people.

Historically, among the Black Church, it has not been uncommon to highlight the parallels between the experiences of Israel and those of African descent in America. Such comparisons fit.

In his book *Troubling Biblical Waters*, Dr. Cain Hope Felder notes, "Blacks have . . . developed an 'experiential sympathy' with much of the Bible, which in turn receives their reverent attention as quite literally the revealed Word of God." In essence Felder is saying that reading the stories of the plight of the biblical people of God has resonated with African Americans. Reading the history of Israel, in ways, has been like reading Black history. They were enslaved and so are we; they cried out to the Lord, so will we. He delivered them, He will deliver us! Songs and sermons that convey these common experiences have been met with a resounding "Amen and amen."

Undeniably, African Americans have a legacy that includes pain. The pain of chattel slavery where forebears were viewed as property. Some years ago I visited the southern county where my grandmother was born. How exhilarating it was to see the record of my great-grandfather's will among the public records. But it was equally painful to see records of the last wishes of members of the majority community, who had at death bequeathed slaves to other family members. It's still quite painful to watch old news footage of African American people being attacked by dogs or with water hoses, or being verbally and physically abused and then arrested simply for wanting to sit down for a meal.

While the things noted here are real and ugly, there is more to this story, more to the African American legacy. Not only has there been real pain but, more often than not, that pain has been countered with real hope, a hope that goes beyond faith in the failed systems of this world. Hope has come because the God of the Bible has made himself known in the person and work of the Lord Jesus Christ.

Felder (cited previously) is right about our developing what we call "experiential sympathy," but please know that experience also includes sharing the hopes of the people of God of old, who saw the Lord as the God who could "make a way out of no way."

My grandmother was a hymn-singing, catechism-reciting Presbyterian. As an infant my mother took me to an African Methodist Episcopalian church where I was baptized. As a teenager I came to personal faith in the Lord Jesus at a Church of God in Christ. As an adult my faith has grown in the context of African American–led churches. African Americans' attendance, participation, and membership in local churches span a wide spectrum of denominations but in those local Christian assemblies, faith has been fueled and strengthened to live in the midst of a world that hasn't always been friendly.

Those who gather to worship today in African American churches stand on the shoulders of those who have stared personal and social dangers, toils, and snares in the face with hope in God's sufficient grace. With these things in mind, the exhortation of the writer to the Hebrews is worth hearing again. The legacy that has been bequeathed is a legacy of "dangers, toils, and snares," but it is also a legacy of hope. African American history features well-known and little-known women and men whose lives are a testimony to God's amazing grace.

So, imagine (as you sit in your favorite pew or seat in your church) that the traditional verses of the beloved "Amazing Grace" have been sung. As often is the case in some of our churches, the song is still not over. The song leader adds a verse that would get an "amen":

> Praise God, praise God, praise God,
>   praise God;
> praise God, praise God, praise God.
> Praise God, praise God; praise God,
>   praise God;
> praise God, praise God, praise God.

Grace has brought us safe thus far, and grace will lead us home!

SHINE

Cherie Trahan

*In the same way, let your light
shine before others, that they
may see your good deeds and
glorify your Father in heaven.*

Matthew 5:16

"This little light of mine... I'm gonna let it
shine," written in the 1920s as a gospel song for
children, transformed into an iconic freedom song.
Activists, including Fannie Lou Hamer, taught the
song to US civil rights demonstrators in the 1960s.
The joyful melody and defiant lyrics sparked courage. In the face of violence that demonstrators suffered, they shouted confidence in God's divine
presence, protection, and power over injustice,
strengthening their hope.

By the time "This Little Light of Mine" reached
me, I was growing up in a Black United Methodist
church. Our children's choir director (using her
signature *loud whisper* during worship services) instructed us to sing and shout confidently: "Every-
where I go, I'm going to let it shine!" This song

was a seed affirming my identity in Christ as *my light*.

With a theme that mirrors Jesus's words to followers, "Let your light shine before others" (Matthew 5:16), we gain that divine calling when we accept Him as our Savior. We will find ourselves on the "front lines," facing challenging life situations. Our rays of hope, joy, love, and compassion encourage us, and pique others' interest. Whether others' reactions to us are wonder, admiration, or unfavorable oppression, our salvation illuminates! The freedom we exhibit in Christ bears witness to Scripture and our unshakable faith in God. We're designed to shine—and others see the light.

> Although the world might try to diminish our light, the world does not have the power to hide what God has lit.

God, help me to keep Your joy and radiate Your Spirit even as I face the challenges that are present in my life, and I will give You all the praise. In Jesus's name, amen.

Matthew 5:1–16

¹Now when Jesus saw the crowds, he went up on a mountainside and sat down. His disciples came to him, ²and he began to teach them.

He said:

³"Blessed are the poor in spirit,
　　for theirs is the kingdom of
　　heaven.
⁴Blessed are those who mourn,
　　for they will be comforted.
⁵Blessed are the meek,
　　for they will inherit the
　　earth.
⁶Blessed are those who hun-
　　ger and thirst for
　　righteousness,
　　for they will be filled.
⁷Blessed are the merciful,
　　for they will be shown
　　mercy.
⁸Blessed are the pure in heart,
　　for they will see God.
⁹Blessed are the peacemakers,
　　for they will be called chil-
　　dren of God.
¹⁰Blessed are those who are
　　persecuted because of
　　righteousness,
　　for theirs is the kingdom of
　　heaven.

¹¹"Blessed are you when people insult
you, persecute you and falsely say all kinds

of evil against you because of me. [12]Rejoice and be glad, because great is your reward in heaven, for in the same way they persecuted the prophets who were before you.

[13]"You are the salt of the earth. But if the salt loses its saltiness, how can it be made salty again? It is no longer good for anything, except to be thrown out and trampled underfoot.

[14]"You are the light of the world. A town built on a hill cannot be hidden. [15]Neither do people light a lamp and put it under a bowl. Instead they put it on its stand, and it gives light to everyone in the house. [16]In the same way, let your light shine before others, that they may see your good deeds and glorify your Father in heaven."

HE WILL NOT FORGET!

Arthur Jackson

God is not unjust; he will not forget your work and the love you have shown him as you have helped his people and continue to help them.

Hebrews 6:10

My first extended road trip was to Memphis, Tennessee, to attend the national convocation of the Churches of God in Christ. Worship services convened at Mason Temple, named in honor of Charles Harrison Mason, the founder of the Churches of God in Christ. Here, Dr. Martin Luther King Jr. delivered his renowned "I've Been to the Mountaintop" speech (it would be King's last).

Bishop Mason's entombed body lies within the building and engraved on his tomb are words from Hebrews 6:10: "For God is not unrighteous to forget your work and labour of love, which ye have shewed toward his name, in that ye have ministered to the saints" (KJV). These words from Scripture encourage our hearts and remind us of several noteworthy truths about God. He is not unjust. Or, to put it another way, He can be trusted. Sooner or later people and systems will fail us, but the Judge of all the earth never fails. He will do right (see Genesis 18:25).

The other amazing truth that encourages our hearts is that the Lord doesn't suffer from amnesia; no memory loss with God! How assuring it is to know that the labors of faithful leaders like Bishop Mason and the diligent work of all who serve the Lord by serving people are deeply embedded in the unfailing memory of God.

God is trustworthy, just, and remembers us.

When I am tempted to forget Your faithfulness, Almighty God, please prompt me to recall all that You are, have done, and will do because of Your love for me, and to share Your love with others.

Hebrews 6:9–12 NLT

⁹Dear friends, even though we are talking this way, we really don't believe it applies to you. We are confident that you are meant for better things, things that come with salvation. ¹⁰For God is not unjust. He will not forget how hard you have worked for him and how you have shown your love to

him by caring for other believers, as you still do. ¹¹Our great desire is that you will keep on loving others as long as life lasts, in order to make certain that what you hope for will come true. ¹²Then you will not become spiritually dull and indifferent. Instead, you will follow the example of those who are going to inherit God's promises because of their faith and endurance.

THIRST AND RESPONSIBILITY

Tondra L. Loder-Jackson

We will tell the next generation the praiseworthy deeds of the LORD.

Psalm 78:4

Born fifteenth of seventeen children in 1875, Mary McLeod Bethune was first in her family to be born free and to become literate. Her Methodist parents valued education, but public schools in Mayesville, South Carolina, did not admit Blacks. So they sent her to Trinity Presbyterian Mission School for Negroes.

Bethune aspired to become a missionary in Africa, but no church was willing to sponsor her. She redirected her zeal to educating Black students in the United States. Mary became the first and only woman to found and serve as president of a historically Black college: Bethune-Cookman University, Daytona Beach, Florida.

Bethune's legacy embodies Asaph's Psalm 78 that shares lessons from Israel's past: "Tell the next generation the praiseworthy deeds of the LORD, his power, and the wonders he has done" (v. 4). This extended to "even the children yet to be born," who were to tell their children (v. 6).

Before she died, Bethune penned "My Last Will and Testament," bequeathing "a thirst for education" and "a responsibility to our young people." She said, "If we have the courage and tenacity of our forebears, who stood firmly like a rock against the lash of slavery, we shall find a way to do for our day what they did for theirs." Bethune foresaw that only by God's praiseworthy deeds and power could Bethune-Cookman educate succeeding generations to persevere and overcome the challenges historically Black colleges and universities (HBCUs) would face.

> What are you facing today that requires
> your responsibility and courage?

Father, thank You for training our generations
in Your Word and for giving us courage.

Psalm 78:1–8

> ¹My people, hear my teaching;
>   listen to the words of my
>   mouth.
> ²I will open my mouth with a
>   parable;

I will utter hidden things,
    things from of old—
³things we have heard and
    known,
    things our ancestors have
    told us.
⁴We will not hide them from
    their descendants;
    we will tell the next
    generation
the praiseworthy deeds of the
    LORD,
    his power, and the wonders
    he has done.
⁵He decreed statutes for Jacob
    and established the law in
    Israel,
which he commanded our
    ancestors
    to teach their children,
⁶so the next generation would
    know them,
    even the children yet to be
    born,
    and they in turn would tell
    their children.
⁷Then they would put their
    trust in God

and would not forget his
     deeds
but would keep his
     commands.
[8]They would not be like their
     ancestors—
a stubborn and rebellious
     generation,
whose hearts were not loyal to
     God,
whose spirits were not faith-
     ful to him.

SHEPHERD'S LOVE

Roslyn Yilpet

Jesus said, "Take care of my sheep."
John 21:16

Dr. Frederick Sampson Jr. embraced everyone he met with a heartwarming smile and uplifting words. While my pastor was known throughout the National Baptist denomination as an exemplary orator, those who knew him called him "Doc" and felt his love. Like a good shepherd, he gently guided his members toward transforming their lives to be more like Jesus. As a Black pastor, Doc didn't hesitate to preach about racism and the injustices experienced by our communities.

Jesus asked Peter three times, "Do you love me?" (John 21:15–17). This question signifies the importance of love as a qualification for shepherding God's people. The shepherd must love Jesus in order to love His sheep. Black pastors who address and care for their community's needs exemplify that love for Jesus means caring about and providing justice for people.

Historian W. E. B. Du Bois described the Black pastor by saying, "The preacher is the most unique personality developed by the Negro American soil. A leader, a politician, an orator, a boss, an intriguer, an idealist—all these." From slavery times to present day, Black pastors, men and women, have shepherded our communities toward freedom. They raised our consciousness toward social justice, education, economic growth, and the civic needs of the people. Through spiritual and social leadership, Black pastors continue to fulfill Jesus's commission to feed and care for people.

> Consider how we can pray for and serve alongside those who care for people.

Thank You, Father, for my pastors who lovingly shepherd my loved ones and me.

John 21:15–19

¹⁵ When they had finished eating, Jesus said to Simon Peter, "Simon son of John, do you love me more than these?"

"Yes, Lord," he said, "you know that I love you."

Jesus said, "Feed my lambs."

¹⁶ Again Jesus said, "Simon son of John, do you love me?"

He answered, "Yes, Lord, you know that I love you."

Jesus said, "Take care of my sheep."

[17]The third time he said to him, "Simon son of John, do you love me?"

Peter was hurt because Jesus asked him the third time, "Do you love me?" He said, "Lord, you know all things; you know that I love you."

Jesus said, "Feed my sheep. [18]Very truly I tell you, when you were younger you dressed yourself and went where you wanted; but when you are old you will stretch out your hands, and someone else will dress you and lead you where you do not want to go." [19]Jesus said this to indicate the kind of death by which Peter would glorify God. Then he said to him, "Follow me!"

SOMEONE HAD TO DO IT

Anthony Cobbs

*Going a little farther, he fell with his face
to the ground and prayed, "My Father,
if it is possible, may this cup be taken
from me. Yet not as I will, but as you will."*

Matthew 26:39

Six-year-old Ruby Bridges' first day at William
Frantz Elementary in Louisiana was historic.
Ruby's escorts were armed US marshals. An angry
mob of men and women nearby, protesting deseg-
regation, hurled hate-filled insults at the child.

Seeing images of this little Black girl facing a
White mob, we might wonder why Ruby's parents
allowed their innocent child to walk into those circumstances. Yet, someone had to integrate the school,
and Ruby was assigned the task. Attending school
was dangerous, no rescue from that would come,
and no one else would attend in her place. This was a
pivotal moment in her life, and in America.

When humanity needed the Savior, Jesus understood His assignment. Though the suffering and

TELL THE STORY

humiliation of crucifixion loomed, Jesus prayed in the garden of Gethsemane, "My Father, if it is possible, may this cup be taken from me" (Matthew 26:39). Despite Jesus's appeal, the Father did not change the plan or alter the outcome. Ruby followed Jesus's approach, recalling later in life: "Somehow, it always worked. Kneeling . . . and talking to the Lord made everything okay."

Enduring hate, betrayal, and pain isn't easy, especially when we have a choice to avoid it. A brave six-year-old and her parents reflect the mindset of Jesus when He conceded, "not as I will, but as you will" (v. 39). That changed the course of humanity. May we strive to be as willing in order to bring about change.

> What is a struggle you may need
> to take to God in prayer?

God, help me to handle adverse situations,
including those I don't want to endure.

Matthew 26:36–46

³⁶Then Jesus went with his disciples to a place called Gethsemane, and he said to them, "Sit here while I go over there and pray." ³⁷He took Peter and the two sons of Zebedee along with him, and he began to be

sorrowful and troubled. [38] Then he said to them, "My soul is overwhelmed with sorrow to the point of death. Stay here and keep watch with me."

[39] Going a little farther, he fell with his face to the ground and prayed, "My Father, if it is possible, may this cup be taken from me. Yet not as I will, but as you will."

[40] Then he returned to his disciples and found them sleeping. "Couldn't you men keep watch with me for one hour?" he asked Peter. [41] "Watch and pray so that you will not fall into temptation. The spirit is willing, but the flesh is weak."

[42] He went away a second time and prayed, "My Father, if it is not possible for this cup to be taken away unless I drink it, may your will be done."

[43] When he came back, he again found them sleeping, because their eyes were heavy. [44] So he left them and went away once more and prayed the third time, saying the same thing.

[45] Then he returned to the disciples and said to them, "Are you still sleeping and resting? Look, the hour has come, and the Son of Man is delivered into the hands of sinners. [46] Rise! Let us go! Here comes my betrayer!"

"RISE UP, SHEPHERD, AND FOLLOW"

Carey H. Latimore IV

There's a star in the East on Christmas morn; rise up, shepherd, and follow; it will lead to the place where Christ was born.

"Rise Up, Shepherd, and Follow"

I remember it as though it were yesterday. We were worshipping at church during our family reunion time in Aiken, South Carolina. At the beginning of the service, the congregation started to sing. Never before in my life had I heard singing so beautiful and distinct. One of the church leaders actually read the lyrics to the song and the congregation sang back the lyrics. I asked my mother, an elementary music teacher, about this music style. *Lining-out,* she called it. I later learned lining-out has not been exclusive to African Americans; even today it can be heard in churches, particularly in

Appalachia, in the Primitive Baptist, and in other traditions.

Lining-out in the historic Black Church began in the era of slavery and Reconstruction when many of these churches had very few congregants who could read. Literate members of a church would read the lyrics and the congregation would respond in song, often changing the style and improvising lyrics, chords, and pitch.

A similar tradition for African Americans is *call and response* that still flourishes in our singing and preaching. Call and response occurs when a leader, often a preacher, deacon, or church elder speaks and the congregation responds. Call and response does not have to occur in a church. As in lining-out, call and response is a sign of the Black community's cultural devotion to participatory democracy that allows *everyone* to contribute to the worship experience.

The singing and preaching traditions in the Black Church demonstrate its ability to be flexible and adapt to people's needs. The spirituals are part of that tradition. The spirituals shared the gospel while transmitting messages that were also social and political. The lyrics of the spirituals could be improvised to fit the needs of the people. These spirituals were inclusive and invited everyone to participate in the worship experience.

Ruth McEnery Stuart, a woman from a prominent

Louisiana family, published the first known version of "Rise Up, Shepherd, and Follow" as part of an essay titled "Christmas Gifts" in *Lippincott's Monthly Magazine*. In this story, which probably reflects her experiences growing up as a young girl in Louisiana, Stuart writes about life on a Louisiana plantation where the slaves sang a song ("Rise Up, Shepherd") during Christmas season. The song is in the call-and-response tradition, as the soloist sings the lead and the congregation follows. This is different from lining-out because the congregation is responding to the soloist and not merely repeating the words.

According to Dr. Eileen Guenther, "Rise Up, Shepherd" is one of the few "Christmas spirituals." We know that Christmas season for slaves was a period of celebration, as masters typically gave their slaves the day off and often presented them with small gifts. In this spiritual, however, we see that the Christmas season meant more to slaves and their descendants than the small gifts they may have shared or received. They saw the season as an opportunity to celebrate the birth of Jesus. And there is a definite evangelical tone to the song, with its strong cadences encouraging them to rise up and follow Jesus, the Savior.

"Rise Up, Shepherd" also reveals to us that slaves knew more about the Bible than we may initially assume. The song begins with "There's a star in the East on Christmas morn. . . . It will lead to the place that Christ was born." Although a relatively simple song to remember, the song is underpinned with theological nuance. For example, in Matthew's gospel, the wise men from the East saw His star and traveled to Jerusalem asking, "Where is the one who has been born king of the Jews? We saw his star when it rose and have come to worship him" (Matthew 2:2).

The Bible does not tell us much about these wise men and "Rise Up, Shepherd" does not expand on Matthew's gospel. The spiritual is faithful to the biblical story with one exception: In Matthew's gospel, it is the wise men who follow the star while in "Rise Up, Shepherd," it is the shepherds who follow the star. If we look at Luke's gospel, we find mention of the shepherds, whom the angels told about Jesus.

> Today in the town of David a Savior has
> been born to you; he is the Messiah, the
> Lord. This will be a sign to you: You will
> find a baby wrapped in cloths and lying
> in a manger. (Luke 2:11–12)

The shepherds heard the message and rose from where they were and went to find Jesus. What explains this discrepancy between the Gospels and the spiritual? Is it possible that these ancestors confused the two stories? I believe that the discrepancy is intentional. If we examine Stuart's earliest version of the song, we see in the first verse after the line about the star and shepherds, in the next solo line: "If you've taken good notice to the angels' words" (for reading clarity I have converted the dialect). While this line is not included in most modern renditions of the song, I believe this line means that the slaves recognized the difference between the wise men and the shepherds. This verse from the song makes clear they were familiar with the details of the shepherds' particular narrative in Luke's gospel. So, it is likely that they intentionally substituted the shepherds in the place of the wise men. I also believe that within references to the shepherds rising up and following lay a hidden message about the North Star, which led thousands of slaves to freedom in the North and even Canada. Since most slaves would find it easier to identify with the shepherds (who, like them, were poor) than rich men, this perhaps served as an incentive to substitute shepherds for wise men.

The lyrics of this spiritual are certainly radical for that time, when one recognizes the lengths to which masters went, often hiring plantation preachers, such as the Reverend Alexander Glennie, to ensure that the gospel that slaves heard was compatible with slave masters' desire to control them. In a time when masters wanted their slaves to focus specifically on biblical interpretations that encouraged slaves' submissiveness, the fact that "Rise Up, Shepherd" survives to this day demonstrates the independence of these slave ancestors. While masters wanted their slaves to submit to them, this spiritual song demonstrates that slaves desired to rise up and follow the Messiah.

This spiritual gives us many takeaways. First, slave resistance to masters and obedience to the Bible were compatible. "Rise Up, Shepherd" also proves our slave ancestors recognized the importance of Jesus's birth. And the slaves' faithfulness to the biblical text demonstrates a stronger adherence to the truth than their masters, who sought to erase the more radical parts of the Bible.

It should not surprise us that slaves found the humble story about Jesus's birth noteworthy. That certainly spoke volumes to a slave that Jesus was the embodiment of the prophet Isaiah's Old Testament prediction foretelling Luke 4:18:

> The Spirit of the Sovereign LORD is on me, because the LORD has anointed me to proclaim good news to the poor. He has sent me to bind up the brokenhearted, to proclaim freedom for the captives and release from darkness for the prisoners. (Isaiah 61:1)

In a society obsessed with wealth and prosperity, the story of Jesus's birth speaks and demonstrates God is unimpressed by simply material gifts. We, too, can strive to recognize Christmas means so much more than gifts and a day off from labors. We enjoy a special opportunity to remember Jesus, the Messiah, who frees us and cleanses our iniquities for time eternal. Indeed, these ancestors demonstrated that they would worship Him in all conditions. What a message for us! Whatever our current situation, there is always plenty of reasons to celebrate the birth of our Lord.

THIS IS US

Barbranda Lumpkins Walls

Let the redeemed of the Lord tell their story—those he redeemed from the hand of the foe, those he gathered from the lands, from east and west, from north and south.

Psalm 107:2–3

I was excited on my first visit to the National Museum of African American History and Culture in Washington, DC. But my joy turned into sorrow as I descended into the museum's depths. I stood and stared at the tiny shackles made for children. I choked back tears at the wall inscribed with names of slaves, each sold for a few dollars. Stories of God's children, who faced incredible hardships, were on display—those whose redemption was bought with the price of Jesus's blood (1 Corinthians 6:20).

The museum revealed the ships bringing human cargo from Africa to America. How a revered US president enslaved people. How Black men who fought for their country were disrespected and denied full citizenship. Leaving that gallery, my spirit lifted as I ascended to the upper floors. I saw how our ancestors believed in God to make a way for them. How they prayed. How they fought for freedom through marches and sit-ins. How they sacrificed to give their children a better life. Their stories of redemption shine light in darkness. We can "give thanks to the Lord, for he is good" (Psalm 107:1).

I reached the top floors—a glorious display of accomplishments—bursting with gratitude at the resolve, resourcefulness, and resilience of African Americans, whom the Lord delivered from unimaginable atrocities to thrive. And through God's grace, our complex and inspiring story continues to evolve for future generations.

> Who in your family or in history causes you to pause and thank God for their courage and sacrifices?

Thank You, God, for Your faithfulness, our redemption, and our deliverance.

Psalm 107:1–9

> [1] Give thanks to the Lord, for
>   he is good;
>   his love endures forever.

²Let the redeemed of the LORD
tell their story—
those he redeemed from the
hand of the foe,
³those he gathered from the
lands,
from east and west, from
north and south.

⁴Some wandered in desert
wastelands,
finding no way to a city
where they could settle.
⁵They were hungry and thirsty,
and their lives ebbed away.
⁶Then they cried out to the
LORD in their trouble,
and he delivered them from
their distress.
⁷He led them by a straight way
to a city where they could
settle.
⁸Let them give thanks to the
LORD for his unfailing
love
and his wonderful deeds for
mankind,
⁹for he satisfies the thirsty
and fills the hungry with
good things.

DEEPER STILL

CJ Rhodes

"Not by might nor by power, but by my Spirit," says the Lord Almighty.

Zechariah 4:6

In 1895, Charles Price Jones had no idea God would use him to ignite a revival. When he came to Jackson, Mississippi, to lead the city's oldest African American congregation, Jones found the members of Mt. Helm Baptist Church and the broader community in disrepair. The civil rights gained following the Civil War were gone. Terrified yet resilient, many Black pastors believed that an organized, educated people could push back against darkness and rebuild.

In Zechariah, the Lord assured the people through the prophet that the temple would, indeed, be rebuilt. But rebuilding, we're told in Zechariah 4:6, wouldn't happen through human agency alone. The Spirit's power, not human power or might, would achieve this great goal.

Jones, a young minister, observed that his Black community in Mississippi's capital city had issues beyond what state house policymakers concocted.

The spiritual life of many church members was dim and rudderless. His own soul yearned for more from God. An encounter with the Holy Spirit convicted Jones that there was more power for victorious living if God's people would cry out for revival. A year later, Jones spearheaded a Holiness convention that in time gave rise to the Church of God in Christ. Souls were saved, bodies healed, and praise resounded from people rejuvenated by God's presence and power.

When we yield ourselves to the Spirit, we're bound to see God do things beyond our wildest dreams.

How is the Spirit inviting you to trust more in God's divine power?

Spirit of the living God, give me inner strength to go deeper.

Zechariah 4:1–6

¹Then the angel who talked with me returned and woke me up, like someone awakened from sleep. ²He asked me, "What do you see?"

I answered, "I see a solid gold lampstand with a bowl at the top and seven lamps on it, with seven channels to the lamps. ³Also there are two olive trees by it, one on the right of the bowl and the other on its left."

⁴I asked the angel who talked with me, "What are these, my lord?"

⁵He answered, "Do you not know what these are?"

"No, my lord," I replied.

⁶So he said to me, "This is the word of the Lord to Zerubbabel: 'Not by might nor by power, but by my Spirit,' says the Lord Almighty."

STEPPING OUT

Lisa D. Robinson

*And what does the L*ORD *require of you? To act justly and to love mercy and to walk humbly with your God.*

Micah 6:8

Septima Poinsette Clark stepped out of her comfort zone for others. Dr. Martin Luther King Jr. referred to Clark as the Mother of the Civil Rights Movement. Born in South Carolina, Septima's mother was a free Black Haitian and her father had been born a slave. At the end of Septima Clark's life, her headstone recorded her steps: "Humanitarian, Civil Rights Activist, Teacher, Leader, Friend." She provided hope to thousands. She led efforts to set up "Citizenship Schools" in the Deep South, to establish literacy for Black adults. Her courageous efforts to empower Blacks led to intense resistance and retaliation, including false arrests, intimidation, and backlash from her employers.

This opposition seemed to increase Clark's desire to seek justice for those in need. Micah's words teach us how to hope in the face of despair, too, and challenge the status quo, in order to do what

God requires. God spoke through Micah to ask the people of Israel the simple question, "And what does the Lord require of you?" God's answer, "To act justly and to love mercy and to walk humbly with your God." These acts are not suggestions, but requirements for true believers.

Clark knew that Black people matter to God. Her acts of resistance to unjust laws and her passion for helping her community inspire us to take steps to create spaces of hope.

> Every day is another chance to do justice and show mercy. How will you choose to walk humbly with God?

Merciful God, thank You for guiding my ancestors during their journey for justice. Help me to walk humbly with You.

Micah 6:1–8

¹ Listen to what the LORD says:

> "Stand up, plead my case before
> the mountains;
>   let the hills hear what you
>   have to say.

²"Hear, you mountains, the
       Lᴏʀᴅ's accusation;
       listen, you everlasting foun-
          dations of the earth.
For the Lᴏʀᴅ has a case against
       his people;
       he is lodging a charge
          against Israel.

³"My people, what have I done
       to you?
       How have I burdened you?
       Answer me.
⁴I brought you up out of Egypt
       and redeemed you from the
          land of slavery.
I sent Moses to lead you,
       also Aaron and Miriam.
⁵My people, remember
       what Balak king of Moab
          plotted
       and what Balaam son of
          Beor answered.
Remember your journey from
       Shittim to Gilgal,
       that you may know the righ-
          teous acts of the Lᴏʀᴅ."

⁶With what shall I come before
       the Lᴏʀᴅ

and bow down before the
exalted God?
Shall I come before him with
burnt offerings,
with calves a year old?
[7]Will the LORD be pleased with
thousands of rams,
with ten thousand rivers of
olive oil?
Shall I offer my firstborn for my
transgression,
the fruit of my body for the
sin of my soul?
[8]He has shown you, O mortal,
what is good.
And what does the LORD
require of you?
To act justly and to love mercy
and to walk humbly with
your God.

EMPTY ME

Santes Beatty

*Do nothing out of selfish ambition
or vain conceit. Rather, in humility
value others above yourselves.*

Philippians 2:3

In the press for freedom, children have borne many costs. Children joined marches, sang Freedom Songs, and ended up in jails during protests for human rights. As an adult, Linda Brown Thompson recalled how her father, a minister in Topeka, Kansas, became one of several plaintiffs in *Brown v. Board of Education*. Parents sought equal access to decent school buildings, books, and supplies. The US Supreme Court tried to remedy some inequities by ending legalized school segregation. However, before her death in 2018, Linda challenged us to consider these results: Black children were uprooted from their welcoming schools, good Black teachers and administrators lost their jobs, and many families suffered immense frustration, ridicule, and isolation. Free education came with sacrifice.

Suffering for others' sake is a common thread in

the beautiful tapestry of God's plan of redemption for all. The faithful sacrifice of some resulting in the benefit of others correlates with Jesus valuing us above himself, taking on the role of a servant. Our Savior put down His divine power, privilege, and position. He bore the cost of our redemption by emptying himself. He modeled this for His followers.

Without Christ's humility, we would not enjoy the freedoms we now have. Are there ways we are willing to suffer for others' sake? Is there something Christ followers need to set down, step away from, or give up, for the greater good?

Jesus Christ humbled himself on our behalf out of love for us, and He has given us His Spirit who encourages and empowers us to empty ourselves on behalf of one another.

God, help me to show gratitude for Your sacrifice for me, and give me courage to humble myself for the sake of others.

Philippians 2:1–11

¹Therefore if you have any encouragement from being united with Christ, if any comfort from his love, if any common sharing in the Spirit, if any tenderness and

compassion, [2]then make my joy complete by being like-minded, having the same love, being one in spirit and of one mind. [3]Do nothing out of selfish ambition or vain conceit. Rather, in humility value others above yourselves, [4]not looking to your own interests but each of you to the interests of the others.

[5]In your relationships with one another, have the same mindset as Christ Jesus:

> [6]Who, being in very nature
>   God,
>   did not consider equal-
>   ity with God something
>   to be used to his own
>   advantage;
> [7]rather, he made himself
>   nothing
>   by taking the very nature of
>   a servant,
>   being made in human
>   likeness.
> [8]And being found in appearance
>   as a man,
>   he humbled himself
>   by becoming obedient to
>   death—
>   even death on a cross!

TELL THE STORY

[9]Therefore God exalted him to
the highest place
and gave him the name that
is above every name,
[10]that at the name of Jesus every
knee should bow,
in heaven and on earth and
under the earth,
[11]and every tongue acknowledge
that Jesus Christ is Lord,
to the glory of God the
Father.

OH, VICTORY

Noel Hutchinson

Therefore, since we are surrounded
by such a great cloud of witnesses, . . .
let us run with perseverance
the race marked out for us.

Hebrews 12:1

In summertime in mid-twentieth-century Black America, many headed from morning worship to the ballpark. Crowds in their Sunday best filled stands at local Negro League games. Black players were barred from the Major League by an unofficial but ironclad color line. That was, until Jackie Robinson broke through—chosen to be the first Negro in the Majors. Robinson entered the big leagues not only because of his skill, now legendary, but also because of perseverance in the face of tension, taunts, and threats that came with being a pioneer for freedom. His success paved the way for others' victories, and his influence was great, including as a strong voice for civil rights.

In Hebrews 11:32–40, culminating with 12:1, we see numerous biblical examples of perseverance active through faith. These persons with

God did some amazing things. Their purposeful walk was outside what we call "success," for even when they didn't achieve their desires, as verse 40 says, "God had planned something better for us so that only together with us would they be made perfect." Our perseverance, encouraged through these witnesses, helps us to complete great challenges begun before us.

When we run the race before us with Christ, we can do the impossible and see victory through the power found in God. What doors will He open through you? The cloud of witnesses looks from the balcony of heaven, cheering for your success.

> There is nothing too hard for God and nothing impossible with God.

God please give me the perseverance I need to fulfill Your plans for my life despite the obstacles that occur, and make my success a visible illustration of Your faithfulness, for Your glory.

Hebrews 11:32–12:1

[32]And what more shall I say? I do not have time to tell about Gideon, Barak, Samson and Jephthah, about David and Samuel and the prophets, [33]who through faith conquered kingdoms, administered

justice, and gained what was promised; who shut the mouths of lions, ³⁴quenched the fury of the flames, and escaped the edge of the sword; whose weakness was turned to strength; and who became powerful in battle and routed foreign armies. ³⁵Women received back their dead, raised to life again. There were others who were tortured, refusing to be released so that they might gain an even better resurrection. ³⁶Some faced jeers and flogging, and even chains and imprisonment. ³⁷They were put to death by stoning; they were sawed in two; they were killed by the sword. They went about in sheepskins and goatskins, destitute, persecuted and mistreated— ³⁸the world was not worthy of them. They wandered in deserts and mountains, living in caves and in holes in the ground.

³⁹These were all commended for their faith, yet none of them received what had been promised, ⁴⁰since God had planned something better for us so that only together with us would they be made perfect.

¹Therefore, since we are surrounded by so great a cloud of witnesses . . . let us run with perseverance the race marked out for us.

WHY WE PRAY WHAT WE PRAY

Marvin Williams

Father, I stretch my hands to Thee. No other help I know. If Thou withdraw Thy help from me, ah, whither shall I go?

"Father, I Stretch My Hands to Thee"

When I was growing up, I was in awe when I listened to my mother and other mothers in our church pray. Sometimes they would sit in silence and whisper words to the Father. Still other times, they would lay themselves down prostrate and weep prayers to God. I watched these saints raise their hands and stretch out their arms as they sang what to them was a familiar hymn by Dr. Watts: "Father, I Stretch My Hands to Thee."

I can still remember the way the room seemed to shake with divine power. God was present. Though I couldn't see Him, I could feel His power when these saints worshiped in prayer. The God of the universe was on the premises, and they talked to and with Him like He was an old best friend sitting right next to them. These old saints would humbly say that they were so close to God that they could feel His breath on them. Listening to them pray with boldness, power, and passion created a longing in my heart to pray this way as well. I wanted what they had. I still do.

The truth is, most days I don't think I come close to praying this way. I struggle to pray. I lose focus, get distracted, feel my life is too busy, and doubt God hears me. Sometimes I even get bored and fall asleep.

So I can find myself slogging through and sweating in my prayer life. I know from my childhood that prayer can be joyful and life-changing. And some days it is. But there are other days when it feels mundane and monotonous. Yet the legacy of faith I experienced as a child still lives in me. I still long to hear the Father tell me who He is, who I am, and where I am going. I still long to experience in prayer the joy only He can give. And when I reflect more deeply on some of the reasons we pray, I am even more motivated to keep pressing on in prayer.

Why do we pray? Out of habit and duty? Do we pray just to get stuff from God? While there's nothing wrong with bringing our needs before God and asking Him to bless us, this is only a small part of the wonder of what we are invited into through the privilege of prayer.

One of the foundational reasons we pray is

because God invites us into the joy of being with Him. Prayer is not a duty, but an invitation from our Father into fellowship with Him through Jesus Christ. Through adoration, thanksgiving, and intercession, we draw near to God and learn more of His will for our spiritual growth. We can accept this invitation and approach the Father, not because we are so good or have all the right words, but because of Jesus's sacrifice. In Him, a new and living way has opened (Hebrews 10:20). His loving sacrifice has given each of us a way to freely access the living God (John 3:16). Through Jesus, we can come to God with freedom and confidence.

As His beloved children in Christ (Ephesians 5:1), through the Spirit we cry out to God as our Father, our *Abba* (Galatians 4:6). When we turn to Him, He has compassion on us, knowing how weak and vulnerable we are (Psalm 103:13–14). Like a good father, through His grace, God gives us things that we do not deserve, while through His mercy shielding us from those things we do deserve (Romans 8:15; Galatians 4:6). Through prayer, we nurture this tender relationship with our Father. By leaning into this relationship, we experience His love while expressing how much we love Him. In the presence of the living God, we are reminded who He is and who we are.

Through the gift of prayer, God not only invites us into an ever-deepening relationship with Him, but He also invites us to experience divine purpose and power through the Holy Spirit, our Comforter and teacher (John 14:26 KJV). As with the saints of old, God invites us to use prayer to accomplish much. He uses our prayers to fight Satan (Luke 22:31–32), restore others (James 5:16), impart wisdom (James 1:5), raise up laborers for the gospel (Matthew 9:38), find peace (Philippians 4:5–7), and heal (James 5:14–15). When we understand that God is inviting us into something precious and powerful—an ever-deepening relationship with Him and access to His power—it's wonderful to receive His invitation. When we see prayer this way, it becomes less of a routine and more joyful anticipation of how our Father will move the world for His glory and our good.

A couple years ago, my oldest son was diagnosed with amblyopia, a condition better known as "lazy eye," in which the vision in one of the eyes is decreased because the eye and the brain are not working together properly. The eye itself looks normal, but it is not being used normally because the brain is favoring the other eye. The doctor said that his vision in one eye was reduced, and he would eventually go blind in that eye. My wife and I called the prayer team at our church, and they gathered around my son and prayed for him. We prayed because God invited us to draw near to the throne of grace that we might receive mercy and find grace in time of need (Hebrews 4:16). We prayed, cried, and trusted. We prayed because God invites us to pray, and when we do, our Father responds to the cries of His children—in the time and in the ways that are best. And in our moment of desperate need, we experienced His power and love and supernatural healing.

The older I get, the more I realize why the prayers of the saints of old in the Black Church were so powerful and effective. They didn't just know *about* God; they knew God *personally*. The why of their prayers preceded the what of their prayers. They prayed, not out of duty, but from their desperate need for His presence and power. They prayed not to get stuff from God, but to get God.

A MELODY OF LOVE

Patricia Raybon

*The stone the builders rejected
has become the cornerstone.*

Psalm 118:22

Her stirring voice brought contralto Marian Anderson worldwide acclaim. Her *race*, however, meant the African American singer often faced hurtful disrespect. One of the worst public rejections was a denial to perform at the famed Constitution Hall in Washington, DC. With help from First Lady Eleanor Roosevelt, however, Anderson was allowed to perform outside on the steps of the Lincoln Memorial. On that Easter Sunday of 1939, a crowd of 75,000 amassed to hear Anderson sing, with millions more listening on radio.

Her biggest achievement, though, was never growing bitter. Instead, she put her faith and focus on God. To Him, she prayed "with the sure knowledge there was Someone to Whom I could pour out the greatest need of my heart and soul." In Him, "I have a freedom in life I could not have in any other way."

　　　　　　　　　TELL THE STORY

The barriers Anderson and all of us face in life invite us to reflect on our Christ, and how He handled rejection.

He is "the stone the builders rejected," but became the "cornerstone" (Psalm 118:22) of our faith. "He was despised and rejected by mankind" (Isaiah 53:3). Yet He served and loved all in dignity, inspiring us to face rejection in the same way. When we do, our lives become transcendent witnesses for God, allowing our hearts to sing freely of Christ with a melody of love.

> Jesus Christ knows all about rejection and upholds our dignity; faith in His overcoming power is sweet inspiration.

Thank You, Lord, for carrying my sorrows, opening doors for me, giving me a praise, and uplifting my heart. In Jesus's name, amen.

Psalm 118:21–23

[21]I will give you thanks, for you answered me;
you have become my salvation.

[22]The stone the builders rejected has become the cornerstone;

^{23}the LORD has done this,
    and it is marvelous in our
        eyes.

FREED, INDEED!

Tondra L. Loder-Jackson

*So if the Son sets you free,
you will be free indeed.*

John 8:36

Renowned Reverend Dr. James H. Cone penned some final thoughts in *The Cross and the Lynching Tree*. The Black Liberation theologian upheld that the cross and tree were symbols of suffering, oppression, and death—intertwining experiences of Black Americans and Jesus Christ.

Cone recalled his childhood in segregated Arkansas: "The violent crosses of the Ku Klux Klan were a familiar reality . . . racists preached a dehumanizing, segregated gospel in the name of Jesus's cross every Sunday." Yet Cone heard a radically different gospel in Black churches: "Preachers proclaimed the message of the suffering Jesus and salvation accomplished in the death on the cross." Cone upheld this gospel truth about freedom: the true message of Christ is that salvation is meant for and validates *all* humans.

Jesus had set the record straight with Jewish leaders identifying themselves as "Abraham's descendants [who] have never been slaves of anyone" (John 8:33). Had they forgotten the Israelites' Egyptian enslavement and Babylonian bondage? Perhaps they were hearkening back to their lineage in Noah's son Shem, blessed by God, and not cursed to slavery as were the children of Noah's son Ham (Genesis 9:18–27)?

Jesus denounced falsehoods that salvation could be obtained (or denied) by birthright, proclaiming: "Everyone who sins is a slave to sin. . . . So if the Son sets you free, you will be free indeed" (John 8:34–36). Salvation depends on Jesus's sacrifice alone.

> God has created us in His image and has set us free from sin through Jesus's sacrifice.

God, help me to walk in the truth of Your Word, reflect Your truth, and display the freedom You have bought with Your life.

John 8:39–47

³⁹"Abraham is our father," they answered.

"If you were Abraham's children," said Jesus, "then you would do what Abraham did. ⁴⁰As it is, you are looking for a way to kill me, a man who has told you the truth that I heard from God. Abraham did not do such things. [41]You are doing the works of your own father."

"We are not illegitimate children," they protested. "The only Father we have is God himself."

[42]Jesus said to them, "If God were your Father, you would love me, for I have come here from God. I have not come on my own; God sent me. [43]Why is my language not clear to you? Because you are unable to hear what I say. [44]You belong to your father, the devil, and you want to carry out your father's desires. He was a murderer from the beginning, not holding to the truth, for there is no truth in him. When he lies, he speaks his native language, for he is a liar and the father of lies. [45]Yet because I tell the truth, you do not believe me! [46]Can any of you prove me guilty of sin? If I am telling the truth, why don't you believe me? [47]Whoever belongs to God hears what God says. The reason you do not hear is that you do not belong to God."

HEAVENLY FREEDOM

Linda Washington

You, my brothers and sisters, were called to be free. But do not use your freedom to indulge the flesh; rather, serve one another humbly in love.

Galatians 5:13

In 1753, at age seven, she was taken from West Africa, brought to Boston, and sold as a slave to John Wheatley for his wife, Susanna. They named the child Phillis. After receiving an education in the Bible, Latin, astronomy, history, and literature, Phillis began writing poetry and eventually became one of the most celebrated poets of this age and the first African American to publish a book. Though eventually set free from slavery, Phillis Wheatley used her poetry and letters to prominent individuals to cry out for "heavenly freedom"—a line from one of her letters— freedom not only for her people but also for the American colonies.

God wanted freedom for His people as well. In Exodus 3, He informed Moses, "I have surely seen

TELL THE STORY

the oppression of My people" (v. 7 NKJV). The Israelites had been enslaved for around 400 years. Though Phillis could only cry out for freedom for her people, God could actually do something to free His. Though the road to freedom would be challenging, Moses's people, like Phillis's, would be free at last.

Phillis died in 1784 before seeing her people freed. Still, she had the joy of witnessing the colonies gain independence from England. She is an example of what the apostle Paul wrote in Galatians 5:13 NLT: "Use your freedom to serve one another in love."

> God cares about the oppressed
> and how we treat them.

Lord, open my eyes to those around me
who need the freedom You provide.

Exodus 3:7–9

[7]The LORD said, "I have indeed seen the misery of my people in Egypt. I have heard them crying out because of their slave drivers, and I am concerned about their suffering. [8]So I have come down to rescue them from the hand of the Egyptians and to bring them up out of that land into a good

and spacious land, a land flowing with milk and honey—the home of the Canaanites, Hittites, Amorites, Perizzites, Hivites and Jebusites. [9]And now the cry of the Israelites has reached me, and I have seen the way the Egyptians are oppressing them.

ENDURING TO CONQUER

Stacy Hawkins Adams

Then Peter came to himself and said, "Now I know without a doubt that the Lord has sent his angel and rescued me from Herod's clutches."

Acts 12:11

In 1965, Amelia Boynton Robinson's image flashed across media. The news images revealed Robinson's painful campaign for freedom to vote. The first African American woman to run for Congress in Alabama in 1964, she participated in a pivotal Civil Rights march from Selma to Alabama's capital, Montgomery. A day before, marcher Jimmie Lee Jackson had been killed.

Among the singing throng of six hundred marchers crossing the Alabama River's Edmund Pettus Bridge, Robinson faced state troopers riding over marchers on horseback, swinging weapons, knocking her and others unconscious. The throng had been singing "Oh, Freedom" and "Come by Here, Lord," but the images capture what is commemorated as "Bloody Sunday." President Lyndon B. Johnson responded to that event by signing the 1965 Voting Rights Act, with Amelia a White House guest.

Jesus's disciple Peter knew the cost of standing up for the freedom Christ offers to all (John 8:36). Imprisoned, awaiting trial, Peter knew King Herod had just murdered another disciple, James. The diverse body of the church at Antioch prayed earnestly for Peter, who was sleeping double-chained, surrounded by Herod's soldiers. And in the darkness, God's shining angel appeared, awoke Peter, and compelled him to a miraculous escape.

Amelia Boynton Robinson's freedom came at a price, and required unwavering faith in the face of painful persecution. Peter's escape reflected commitment to the spiritual freedom Christ gives us, and that God's plans prevail in believers' lives.

> While we're planning our plans, God has already worked out His.

God, thank You for my faith in Your plans and perfect will to prevail in my life and in Your world.

Acts 12:1–10 NLT

¹About that time King Herod Agrippa began to persecute some believers in the

church. [2]He had the apostle James (John's brother) killed with a sword. [3]When Herod saw how much this pleased the Jewish people, he also arrested Peter. (This took place during the Passover celebration.) [4]Then he imprisoned him, placing him under the guard of four squads of four soldiers each. Herod intended to bring Peter out for public trial after the Passover. [5]But while Peter was in prison, the church prayed very earnestly for him.

[6]The night before Peter was to be placed on trial, he was asleep, fastened with two chains between two soldiers. Others stood guard at the prison gate. [7]Suddenly, there was a bright light in the cell, and an angel of the Lord stood before Peter. The angel struck him on the side to awaken him and said, "Quick! Get up!" And the chains fell off his wrists. [8]Then the angel told him, "Get dressed and put on your sandals." And he did. "Now put on your coat and follow me," the angel ordered.

[9]So Peter left the cell, following the angel. But all the time he thought it was a vision. He didn't realize it was actually happening. [10]They passed the first and second guard posts and came to the iron gate leading to the city, and this opened for them all by

itself. So they passed through and started walking down the street, and then the angel suddenly left him.

INVALUABLE TEACHERS

Roslyn Yilpet

*But as for you, continue in what
you have learned and have become
convinced of, because you know
those from whom you learned it.*

2 Timothy 3:14

Society sometimes minimizes the invaluable contributions of Black educators. From Charlotte Forten Grimke, who taught freed slave children during the Civil War, to Mary McLeod Bethune, the founder of Bethune-Cookman University, who set educational standards for today's Black colleges, Black educators have transformed the lives of Black and non-Black students.

The apostle Paul and Timothy's relationship as teacher and student was transformative. Paul modeled to Timothy how to grow his faith: "But as for you, continue in what you have learned and have become convinced of, because you know those from whom you learned it" (2 Timothy 3:14). He instructed Timothy to treasure Scripture and life lessons learned from forebears. Similarly, we can continue applying and teaching our generations what our great Black educators have passed on to generations.

Mrs. Calloway, my ninth-grade typing teacher, taught me more than typing. As a Black woman educator, she instilled in me a desire for moral character and eternal values. She nurtured and inspired her students to break through stereotypical expectations and systemic barriers. Mrs. Calloway's love for her students went beyond the classroom. Years after I graduated, she continued to mentor and support me in my purpose. Even on her deathbed, over fifty years after my high school days, she encouraged me to continue in my faith and challenged me to write about God's faithfulness. God has gifted us with educators who live out His Word.

Throughout history, Black educators have been tireless advocates for our wellness.

God, we thank You and ask Your blessings on those who nurture us in Your Word and model Your character.

2 Timothy 3:14–17

[14]But as for you, continue in what you have learned and have become convinced

of, because you know those from whom you learned it, [15]and how from infancy you have known the Holy Scriptures, which are able to make you wise for salvation through faith in Christ Jesus. [16]All Scripture is God-breathed and is useful for teaching, rebuking, correcting and training in righteousness, [17]so that the servant of God may be thoroughly equipped for every good work.

HBCUS WORLDWIDE WITNESS

Marvin A. McMickle

*But let justice roll on like a river,
righteousness like a never-failing stream!*

Amos 5:24

Cornel West writes, "Prophetic beings have as
their special aim to shatter deliberate ignorance
and willful blindness to the sufferings of others,
and to expose the clever forms of evasion and escape we devise in order to hide and conceal injustice" (*Democracy Matters*). It would be impossible
to discuss the legacies of historically Black colleges
and universities (HBCUs) without referring to the
many bold leaders of the Civil Rights Movement,
who raised their voices for justice to overcome people's sufferings. These leaders have had an impact
on lives around the world. Many were either current students or recent alumni of HBCUs.

From the *Brown v. Board of Education* decision

by the United States Supreme Court in 1954 to the passage of the Civil Rights Bill in 1964, and the Voting Rights Act of 1965, HBCUs produced an incredible number of persons who were instrumental in those events that "let justice roll" (Amos 5:24). And it was not just students who made a contribution, but many of the HBCUs encouraged, supported, protected, and occasionally accommodated protests against injustice that students participated in.

Thurgood Marshall was lead attorney for the National Association for the Advancement of Colored People (NAACP) in the *Brown v. Board of Education* decision declaring segregation in public education unconstitutional. That 1954 ruling essentially overturned *Plessy v. Ferguson*, the 1896 US Supreme Court ruling that had established racial segregation as constitutional, enforcing "separate but equal" discrimination. That had forced Blacks to separate restrooms, drinking fountains, seating in the back of the bus, and more "Jim Crow" injustices. Marshall, the great-grandson of a slave, graduated from Maryland's Colored High School (later named Frederick Douglass High School) in Baltimore and went on to HBCU Lincoln University, and then earned his law degree from Howard University School of Law.

The dean of that law school was Charles Hamilton Houston, who trained his students who would be attorneys to see themselves as architects of social change. That is exactly what Marshall continued in his career, as US Solicitor General, and then first African American member of the United States Supreme Court in 1967. Marshall's church rector said of Marshall, "The Spirit working through this man gave him an intuitive sense of justice in which he saw all of life as sacred and all persons equal before God" (*Relevant Magazine*).

Rev. Dr. Martin Luther King Jr., who graduated from Morehouse College in Atlanta, Georgia, on the heels of the Brown decision, spearheaded the Montgomery Bus Boycott in Alabama, 1955 to 1956, challenging segregation in public transportation. King and others organized the Southern Christian Leadership Conference (SCLC) in 1957, and many founding members and eventual leaders of that organization were graduates of HBCUs. King's fight for justice for all is well documented. Many others worked alongside King, including Rev. Ralph Abernathy. Abernathy had joined the army after high school, then gained his bachelor's degree from Alabama State University, Montgomery, and his master's from Atlanta University. Abernathy helped create the Montgomery Improvement Association that led to the pivotal Montgomery bus boycotts while serving as a pastor, and as dean of students at Alabama State.

Also working with King were Dr. Andrew Young,

who became executive director of the SCLC after King's death. Young had attended Dillard University, New Orleans, Louisiana, and graduated Howard. He worked alongside King and Abernathy, and with the National Council of Churches, on voter registration and education. Young helped draft the 1964 Civil Rights Act and the Voting Rights Act of 1965 and became a three-term congressman from Georgia, an ambassador to the United Nations, and a mayor of Atlanta. He also served his communities as a pastor. Rev. Dr. Wyatt Tee Walker was a graduate of Virginia State University and became a strategist for the Civil Rights Movement. Walker helped found the Congress of Racial Equality, and plan the 1963 March on Washington.

Rev. Fred Shuttlesworth attended Selma University and graduated from Alabama State University in Montgomery. He taught others nonviolent tactics and fought racism and segregation as he pastored in Birmingham, Alabama. He was a co-founder of the SCLC and an advocate for the poor. Hosea Williams was also a member of King's inner circle. He helped lead what became known as the "Bloody Sunday" march in Selma to seek voting rights. After time in the army, Williams had graduated Morris Brown College and earned his masters from Clark Atlanta University. Bernard Lee was a student at Alabama State University in Montgomery until he was expelled for leading part of the student body on a protest march to the Alabama State Capitol in Montgomery. He later attended Morris Brown College in Atlanta. James Bevel attended the American Baptist Theological Seminary in Nashville, Tennessee. Jesse Jackson was a graduate of North Carolina A&T University in Greensboro, North Carolina.

The same was true when the Student Non-Violent Coordinating Committee (SNCC) was founded in 1960 on the campus of Shaw University in Raleigh, North Carolina. C.T. Vivian, Bernard Lafayette, and John Lewis were graduates of American Baptist College in Nashville, Tennessee. Diane Nash graduated from Fisk University, also in Nashville. Marian Wright (Edelman) was a graduate of Spelman College in Atlanta, Georgia. Stokely Carmichael was a graduate of Howard in Washington, DC. SNCC took on two separate and distinct roles during the Civil Rights Movement. The first was the Freedom Rides where Black and White passengers challenged segregation in seating on interstate bus routes. Their second focus was on voter registration in the states of Alabama and Mississippi, especially during the summer of 1964, which they called Freedom Summer. It was during that summer that three civil rights workers—Andrew Goodman, Michael Schwerner, and James Goodman—were murdered in Neshoba County, Mississippi.

HBCUs played a central role in yet another target of the Civil Rights Movement. The sit-ins of 1960 and 1961 sparked the beginning of the student-led efforts of the Civil Rights Movement. Those sit-ins were led by students from two different cities: Nashville, Tennessee, and Greensboro, North Carolina. Those movements included students from North Carolina A&T, American Baptist College, Tennessee State University, and Fisk University. Their peaceful protests involved sitting at lunch counters in various Woolworth's Department Stores before being taunted, beaten, and finally taken to jail. Their objective was to challenge segregation in public accommodations like restaurants and convenience store lunch counters.

Many of the intellectual leaders of the Civil Rights Movement were graduates of HBCUs. William Edward Burghardt Du Bois was a graduate of Fisk University. Howard Thurman was a graduate of Morehouse College. Benjamin Elijah Mays was President of Morehouse College. Samuel DeWitt Proctor, who was a graduate of Virginia Union University in Richmond, Virginia, went on to become president of that school and then became president of North Carolina A&T during the years of the student sit-ins that swept across that campus. In fact, Jesse Jackson was student body president during the time that Dr. Proctor was president of the university. Lawrence Jones, who was dean of the chapel at Fisk University in Nashville, Tennessee, during the sit-ins in that city, was a graduate of West Virginia State University. Septima Poinsette Clark graduated from both Benedict College in Columbia, South Carolina, and Hampton University in Hampton, Virginia.

It should not go unnoticed that at least half of the persons named here were preachers, and others had been training for careers in Christian ministry before their lives took on a different direction. This means that HBCUs were able to train, motivate, equip, and then celebrate the careers of some of the most outstanding preachers and public servants of the twentieth and twenty-first centuries. They helped give meaning to Proverbs 22:6 NKJV, "Train up a child in the way he should go, and when he is old he will not depart from it."

MAKING GOOD TROUBLE

Noel Hutchinson

*Then they called them in again and
commanded them not to speak or
teach at all in the name of Jesus.*

Acts 4:18

The man sat outside the temple on a pallet; his torso sturdy but his legs useless. Given his circumstances, he worked the only occupation available to him—begging. Jesus's followers Peter and John, through God's power, healed the man, giving him the ability to walk. Immediately, everything for this man improved. Some in the temple took exception to this healing, and after Peter and John said it happened through the power of Jesus Christ, the temple leaders ordered them not to preach or teach in His name. They had just stirred up good trouble, trouble created by doing the right thing in an unjust world.

On Sunday, March 17, 1965, some six hundred civil rights marchers gathered in self-determination, dressed in their Sunday best, gaining strength through prayer to walk toward empowerment. They reached the Edmund Pettus Bridge in Selma, Alabama, on their way to register to vote. John Lewis was among the throng. The officers at the other end of the bridge attacked and almost ended the life of Lewis and many others. But the event was instrumental in the passage of the Voting Rights Act. In later years, Lewis gave the template of moving for a just cause, saying "Never, ever be afraid to make some noise and get in good trouble, necessary trouble."

Good trouble anchors in the greater good, going beyond personal comfort, enabling us to change the world through the power of God.

> We are the better for those who have stood up for good in the face of evil.

Father, help me as I pray and we pray, follow Your commands, and serve in the name of Jesus.

Acts 4:18–30

[18]Then they called them in again and commanded them not to speak or teach at all in the name of Jesus. [19]But Peter and John replied, "Which is right in God's eyes: to listen to you, or to him? You be the

judges! ²⁰As for us, we cannot help speaking about what we have seen and heard."

²¹After further threats they let them go. They could not decide how to punish them, because all the people were praising God for what had happened. ²²For the man who was miraculously healed was over forty years old.

²³On their release, Peter and John went back to their own people and reported all that the chief priests and the elders had said to them. ²⁴When they heard this, they raised their voices together in prayer to God. "Sovereign Lord," they said, "you made the heavens and the earth and the sea, and everything in them. ²⁵You spoke by the Holy Spirit through the mouth of your servant, our father David:

> "'Why do the nations rage
>   and the peoples plot in vain?
> ²⁶The kings of the earth rise up
>   and the rulers band together
> against the Lord
>   and against his anointed
>   one.'

²⁷Indeed Herod and Pontius Pilate met together with the Gentiles and the people of Israel in this city to conspire against your holy servant Jesus, whom you anointed.

[28]They did what your power and will had decided beforehand should happen. [29]Now, Lord, consider their threats and enable your servants to speak your word with great boldness. [30]Stretch out your hand to heal and perform signs and wonders through the name of your holy servant Jesus."

MORE THAN A VICTIM

Michelle R. Loyd-Paige

*The Spirit of the Sovereign Lord
is on me, because the Lord has
anointed me to proclaim good news
to the poor. He has sent me to bind
up the brokenhearted, to proclaim
freedom for the captives and release
from darkness for the prisoners.*

Isaiah 61:1

"Ain't I a woman?" abolitionist and former slave Sojourner Truth challenged in 1851, to up-end cultural notions of racial and gender inferiority. In her lecture at a women's rights conference, Truth wasn't asking, but delivering her famous words to express that she was free, and not a victim. Eight years before her speech, she avowed that God had called her to preach the truth and renamed herself Sojourner Truth. Her speech was one of the many ways she fulfilled God's calling on her to proclaim freedom for African Americans and women.

In Isaiah 61:1, we find the prophetic words Jesus would deliver as he spoke in a synagogue in Nazareth on the Sabbath (Luke 4:14–24). In this passage the words *poor*, *brokenhearted*, *captives*, *prisoners* describe the wounded, marginalized, and oppressed among us—or us. Or in other words, victims. Victims of broken relationships, unethical leaders, and corrupt societal systems. To the poor, brokenhearted, captives, and prisoners, Jesus's words meant freedom. His words meant that their sorrows and brokenness had been heard by God and God, not flawed human leaders, would be their deliverer. God, not corrupt and broken justice systems, would bind their wounds and release them from darkness.

Jesus's proclamation of freedom wasn't just for those gathered in the synagogue that day; his proclamation of freedom is for us today.

God, despite corruption in people and systems, is able to reverse and transform situations and free people in every way.

Holy God, please grant me the power to pray for Your will to be done and to speak Your truth that affirms Your will for our freedom.

TELL THE STORY

¹⁴Jesus returned to Galilee in the power of the Spirit, and news about him spread through the whole countryside. ¹⁵He was teaching in their synagogues, and everyone praised him.

¹⁶He went to Nazareth, where he had been brought up, and on the Sabbath day he went into the synagogue, as was his custom. He stood up to read, ¹⁷and the scroll of the prophet Isaiah was handed to him. Unrolling it, he found the place where it is written:

> ¹⁸"The Spirit of the Lord is on
>   me,
>   because he has anointed me
>   to proclaim good news to
>   the poor.
> He has sent me to proclaim
>   freedom for the prisoners
>   and recovery of sight for the
>   blind,
> to set the oppressed free,
>   ¹⁹to proclaim the year of the
>   Lord's favor."

²⁰Then he rolled up the scroll, gave it back to the attendant and sat down. The

eyes of everyone in the synagogue were fastened on him. [21] He began by saying to them, "Today this scripture is fulfilled in your hearing."

[22] All spoke well of him and were amazed at the gracious words that came from his lips. "Isn't this Joseph's son?" they asked.

[23] Jesus said to them, "Surely you will quote this proverb to me: 'Physician, heal yourself!' And you will tell me, 'Do here in your hometown what we have heard that you did in Capernaum.'"

[24] "Truly I tell you," he continued, "no prophet is accepted in his hometown."

LIVING OUR WORDS

Marlena Graves

Let your light shine before others,
that they may see your good deeds
and glorify your Father in heaven.

Matthew 5:16

At six years old, Frederick Douglass was sold and separated from his mother, who was a field hand. He later hypothesized that his father was the White planter who enslaved her. Douglass clearly remembered the horrors and inhumanity that his loved ones were subjected to and spent his life recounting his own trials as a slave. Douglass escaped his enslavement in Maryland and eventually wrote five autobiographies about his life as a slave along with other papers and spoke widely as an abolitionist before and during the Civil War.

Because of the many atrocities and humiliations Douglass experienced and witnessed, he spoke out against slavery on the basis of Scripture. Establishing his antislavery arguments, he made this and other observations: "I love the pure, peaceable, and impartial Christianity of Christ. . . ." And he added, "Therefore, I hate the corrupt, slaveholding, women-whipping, cradle-plundering, partial and hypocritical Christianity of this land."

It's a wonder that Douglass remained a Christian in word and in deed. Inspired by Scripture, Douglass tirelessly traveled to persuade White Christians of the horrors of slavery while fighting to free his people. Like Douglass, let us ask God for strength to live out what we profess. Let us love our neighbors, and enemies, as ourselves so that our lights might shine and onlookers might give glory to God.

> As I look within, can I discern any areas of my life where I need the help of the Spirit to better reflect the truth of the gospel?

Holy Spirit, help us have a healthy Christian community, so that onlookers consider the truths of the gospel by what they observe in us.

Matthew 5:3–16

> 3 Blessed are the poor in spirit,
>   for theirs is the kingdom of
>   heaven.
> 4 Blessed are those who mourn,
>   for they will be comforted.

⁵Blessed are the meek,
>   for they will inherit the
>   earth.
⁶Blessed are those who hun-
>   ger and thirst for
>   righteousness,
>   for they will be filled.
⁷Blessed are the merciful,
>   for they will be shown
>   mercy.
⁸Blessed are the pure in heart,
>   for they will see God.
⁹Blessed are the peacemakers,
>   for they will be called chil-
>   dren of God.
¹⁰Blessed are those who are
>   persecuted because of
>   righteousness,
>   for theirs is the kingdom of
>   heaven.

¹¹Blessed are you when people insult you, persecute you and falsely say all kinds of evil against you because of me. ¹²Rejoice and be glad, because great is your reward in heaven, for in the same way they persecuted the prophets who were before you.

¹³You are the salt of the earth. But if the salt loses its saltiness, how can it be made salty again? It is no longer good for

anything, except to be thrown out and trampled underfoot.

¹⁴You are the light of the world. A town built on a hill cannot be hidden. ¹⁵Neither do people light a lamp and put it under a bowl. Instead they put it on its stand, and it gives light to everyone in the house. ¹⁶In the same way, let your light shine before others, that they may see your good deeds and glorify your Father in heaven.

"WHEN SPIDER WEBS UNITE"

Noel Hutchinson

When you hear them sound a long blast on the trumpets, have the whole army give a loud shout; then the wall of the city will collapse and the army will go up, everyone straight in.

Joshua 6:5

Sometimes the day laborer, housekeeper, and janitor are seen yet unseen. In December 1955, the world saw common folk bring segregation to its knees in the city of Montgomery, Alabama. City officials had arrested Rosa Parks for sitting in the "Whites Only" section of a public bus. For the bus company, this was business as usual, but the common people were tired of that mistreatment. For 381 days, they wore out shoe leather around their "Jericho," segregated city buses, refusing segregated comfort for the rigors of stepping toward unrealized justice.

Evenings found them together for mass meetings in Black churches, hearing strategy, and echoing songs from long ago, and a new one, "We Are Soldiers in the Army," to gain courage while pressing forward. The common people won—buses desegregated—and were a catalyst to the Civil Rights Movement.

An Ethiopian proverb says, "When spider webs unite, they can tie up a lion." When God renewed His promise first made to Moses, He told Joshua and the Israelites to bring Jericho's walls down by walking (see Joshua 6:2–5). His promise extended to "every place where you set your foot" (Joshua 1:3). Unified in obedience to God, an army of former slaves gained victory over one of the most formidable cities of that day. Israelite masses pressed forward together, playing their music and shouting aloud. God still gives improbable victories to united common folk today.

In your experience, in your family, church community, or neighborhood, how has unifying with others in obedience to God brought about good change?

Holy God, thank You for Your enduring promises to me as Your child, and for their instruction to my life and others in hard times and good.

Joshua 1:1–5

¹After the death of Moses the servant of the LORD, the LORD said to Joshua son of Nun, Moses' aide: ²"Moses my servant is dead. Now then, you and all these people, get ready to cross the Jordan River into the land I am about to give to them—to the Israelites. ³I will give you every place where you set your foot, as I promised Moses. ⁴Your territory will extend from the desert to Lebanon, and from the great river, the Euphrates—all the Hittite country—to the Mediterranean Sea in the west. ⁵No one will be able to stand against you all the days of your life. As I was with Moses, so I will be with you; I will never leave you nor forsake you."

FOLLOWING AN UNSEEN PATH

B. Williams Waters

*"For I know the plans I have
for you," declares the LORD.*
Jeremiah 29:11

Seven generations of my family have united
with the African Methodist Episcopal (AME)
Church Richard Allen founded more than two
hundred years ago. So, I knew who Allen was,
about his accomplishments, and the milestones of
his life. Yet it was not until I took a closer look that
I realized something more. The path that led Richard Allen from slavery to founder of a church was
not happenstance; this was God's plan for his life.

When Israel was captive in Babylon, the prophet
Jeremiah wrote a letter affirming God's promise to
bring them out of bondage and assuring them of
God's plans "to prosper you and not to harm you,
plans to give you hope and a future" (Jeremiah
29:11). God has plans for us, too, but it is often
in retrospect that we gain glimpses of these plans.

When Allen bought his freedom, did he know

he would lead others to religious freedom? As he fought for justice, did Allen know his actions would inspire succeeding generations, even as they fought for justice? No, he didn't know. How could he? You see, God's plans for Richard Allen's life unfolded along an unseen path.

We may not know how God's plans will reveal themselves in our lives, or what paths we should take; that's okay. The lives of Richard Allen and others reveal that God's plans for us become fulfilled as we trust Him to lead us along an unseen path.

> How does the assurance that God has plans for your life bring you hope?

God, help me to trust in You and Your Word when I cannot find my way and when I do.

Jeremiah 29:10–14

[10]This is what the LORD says: "When seventy years are completed for Babylon, I will come to you and fulfill my good promise to bring you back to this place. [11]For I know the plans I have for you," declares the LORD, "plans to prosper you and not to harm you, plans to give you hope and a future. [12]Then you will call on me and come and pray to me, and I will listen to

you. ¹³You will seek me and find me when you seek me with all your heart. ¹⁴I will be found by you," declares the LORD, "and will bring you back from captivity. I will gather you from all the nations and places where I have banished you," declares the LORD, "and will bring you back to the place from which I carried you into exile."

THE BIRTH OF AFRICAN AMERICAN DENOMINATIONS

Marvin A. McMickle

*[In Christ] there is neither Jew
nor Gentile, neither slave nor free,
nor is there male and female, for
you are all one in Christ Jesus.*

Galatians 3:28

Despite events of rejection, restriction, and limitation, the historic Black Church in America celebrates a legacy that provides a strong witness to God's faithfulness. We are people of God's grace through the blood of Jesus Christ, kept by the power of His Holy Spirit, encouraged by the promises of Scripture, and people embracing fellowship with fellow Christian believers around the world.

Two events significant to the birth of the historic Black Church denominations in America occurred in Philadelphia, Pennsylvania, in the summer of 1787. The first event was the signing of the United States Constitution that begins with the words, "We the people of the United States." That phrase, "We the people," leads us to the second event that occurred in the same city and in the same year.

A group of African American members of St. George Methodist Episcopal Church went to worship on a certain Sunday morning in 1787. As they entered the sanctuary, they heard the worship leader say, "Let us pray." In traditional Methodist Episcopal custom, they knelt in the aisle of the sanctuary to pray. Suddenly a church usher approached and told them that they could not pray on the first floor of the sanctuary. Instead, they would have to get up and go to the "colored gallery" reserved for so-called "colored" attendees.

Led by Richard Allen and Absalom Jones, the worshippers assured the usher that they would proceed to their assigned location as soon as the morning prayer was over. They reminded the usher that he was creating more of a distraction at that moment than they were. But the usher would not relent. He began to physically pull them from their knees to force them to move. At that moment, and without any prior coordination or agreement, Allen and Jones and the others with them turned around and walked out of the church. Allen concluded in his autobiography, "They were no more plagued with us."

In that moment in 1787, two significant things occurred. First, the seeds were planted for what would become the first Black Church denomination in the history of the United States: the African Methodist Episcopal Church. These believers simply desired to worship God, unhindered, "in the Spirit and in truth" (John 4:23), and founded the new denomination to do so. It would be formed officially in 1816 with Richard Allen as its first bishop.

A second thing that grew out of the walkout from the St. George Methodist Episcopal Church was its immediate challenge to the phrase "we the people of the United States." The US Constitution, in fact, clearly did not apply to African American people. Not to the free African American population of Philadelphia—or to the hundreds of thousands of men, women, and children held in slavery and disregarded around the nation. Though God had created all humans in His divine image (Genesis 1:27) and called all people to love Him and one another (Luke 10:27), the United States did not even validate African Americans as fellow human beings.

The same nation born out of a Revolutionary War to gain freedom and independence from what it deemed to be British oppression and denial of rights, wrote into its constitution protections for chattel slavery (Article 1 section 9). That same nation allowed the transatlantic slave trade to continue for another twenty years, despite the valiant efforts of abolitionists, male and female—African, African American, European, and European American.

US law upheld slavery, and runaway slaves were to be forcibly returned to owners no matter where they were in the country (Article 4 section 2). Those persons held in slavery were counted as only 3/5ths of a person, and that was only to determine taxation and Congressional representation for slave-holding states (Article 1 section 3).

The treatment of African American worshippers in Philadelphia in 1787 opposed the principles of equality that the opening lines of the US Constitution prescribe.

Beginning with the African Methodist Episcopal Church, African American denominations formed because the *we* in "we the people of the United States" in practice did not include African Americans. And the biblical truth of equality in Christ—as expressed by the apostle Paul in his epistle to the Galatians, that "there is neither Jew nor Gentle, neither slave nor free, nor is there male and female, for you are all one in Christ Jesus" (3:28)—did not inform the practices inside St. George Methodist Episcopal Church in 1787.

African American members were forced to worship in a segregated section of the church, or end their worship.

Marginalizing Black worshippers was also the practice at the John Street Methodist Episcopal Church in New York City when James Varick and other African American worshippers walked out of that church in 1796. That led to the formation of the African Methodist Episcopal Zion Church, officially formed in 1821.

In Jackson, Tennessee, in 1870, European American members urged African American members out of the Southern Methodist Episcopal Church, though they assisted the African Americans in the creation of the Colored Methodist Episcopal Church under the leadership of Isaac Lane. The process was different than that of the AME and AME Zion experiences, but the result was the same—despite the Constitution's words, "we the people," and despite God's Word.

Within the life of the Baptist Church in the United States, in 1895 the National Baptist Convention was founded in Atlanta, Georgia, under the leadership of Elias Camp Morris. This was the first of several African American Baptist denominations. It had formed because of African Americans being excluded both from the full fellowship and from any aspect of the leadership of the Northern or Southern Baptist Conventions. "Negroes" could be members of Baptist churches, but they could not hold any office in any state or national conventions. Their churches were free to purchase material from the Baptist publishing house, but no "Negro" could submit any material for publication.

Within the ranks of the Pentecostal Church, the Church of God in Christ (COGIC) was founded in 1897, by African Americans Charles Price Jones and Charles Harrison Mason, as a holiness movement. It began when Mason and Jones were expelled from the National Baptist Convention when the Baptists were not responsive to the holiness emphasis being pursued and pushed by Mason and Jones, which included a belief that complete sanctification and holiness should occur to the believer as a second act of grace in the process of salvation.

C. H. Mason decided to travel to Los Angeles, California, in 1907 to attend the Azusa Street revival being led by William Joseph Seymour. Afterwards, Mason became the only person who attended Azusa Street who also had the authority to ordain persons into the ministry due to COGIC being incorporated by the state of Tennessee. As a result, hundreds of White ministers sought ordination through Mason's leadership. At that moment, the oneness in Christ that had eluded Christians in the United States seemed possible.

However, C. P. Jones rejected the insistence on a "pentecostal experience" as an essential step for salvation. Jones split from Mason, and he went on to form The Church of Christ Holiness USA. In 1914 the White pastors within COGIC, numbering more than three hundred fifty, left to form the Assemblies of God. This occurred for two reasons: worship style differences, and challenges over who would become the predominant leader.

Despite restrictions and limitations, the African American church has emerged as one of the most vibrant locations of praise and worship to be found anywhere in the world today. Their rich heritage of worship began during the days of slavery with what were called "brush harbors" or "hush harbors"—isolated, secret locations where slaves would gather at night for hours of prayer and singing without fear of being heard. Those secret gatherings gave birth to the musical genre known as "Negro spirituals" that wedded both their sorrows and their faith into lyrics like "Nobody knows de trouble I've seen . . . Glory, hallelujah."

Other musical forms and gifted singers have also come from the African American church. The hymns of Charles A. Tindley, James Weldon Johnson, Thomas A. Dorsey, Lucy Campbell, and the songs of Mahalia Jackson, The Winans, Richard Smallwood, Donnie McClurkin, Yolanda Adams, Mississippi Mass Choir, and many more are known and celebrated all over the world.

The power and rhythm of African American

preaching are equally well regarded. Beginning with slave preachers like John Jasper and continuing through such notable voices as Benjamin Elijah Mays and his student Martin Luther King Jr, as well as C. L. Franklin, Gardner Taylor, Vashti Murphy McKenzie, and Kirbyjon Caldwell, to name only a few. African American preachers have ministered to the needs of the brokenhearted, to the sins of a broken nation, and to leaders and people all over the world. And their churches have become central cultural institutions for education, training, and other human services, as well as for civil rights activism.

African American missionaries have put feet and hands to their worship not only by praying and singing but by serving in the United States and across the world. John Marrant served the Native American People. George Liele headed to the Caribbean to help plant a church in Kingston, Jamaica. David George served in Nova Scotia and planted the first Baptist church for Blacks in Silver Bluff, North Carolina. Prince Williams planted churches in the Bahamas. Lott Carey, a former slave, became America's first missionary to Africa. William Henry Shepherd went to the heart of the Congo to preach, provide medical aid, and more. And a growing number of independent churches and denominations performed missions at home to congregants soaring into the tens of millions of African Americans.

African American Christian educators Nannie

TELL THE STORY

Helen Burroughs, Mary McLeod Bethune, Kelly Miller, William Augustus Jones, Gardner C. Taylor, and so many others served to establish educational institutions, including the dozens of Historically Black Colleges and Universities begun by Christians.

From Christian folk artists to celebrated visionaries, African Americans have helped and continue to help beautify the world. James Weldon Johnson's classic poem, "The Creation," and his song, "Lift Ev'ry Voice and Sing" (The Negro National Anthem) prevail across denominations. Biblical artist Henry Ossawa Tanner ("The Banjo Maker"; "The Thankful Poor"; "Daniel in the Lions' Den"; "Jesus Visiting Nicodemus") is celebrated the world over. If a door closed at one venue, God opened the door at another for the use of African Americans' gifts.

God has given African American denominations, churches, and individuals cause to celebrate the legacies He has provided. From African Christian roots to American brush harbors, to the wood-framed buildings of rural communities, from the storefront churches and Gothic cathedrals of the urban landscape, to modern metropolitan complexes, African American denominations, churches, and people have cause to praise and hope. "Let the church say, amen!"

SITTING DOWN TO STAND UP

Santes Beatty

Then Caleb silenced the people before Moses and said, "We should go up and take possession of the land, for we can certainly do it."

Numbers 13:30

They sat down to order, taking an incredible risk. The four freshmen from North Carolina Agricultural and Technical State University wanted more than a cup of coffee. They joined organizers participating in a peaceful protest, a "sit-in" at the local Woolworth's. Eyewitness accounts describe the ferocious verbal and physical attacks these freshmen endured on February 1, 1960, for doing what people take for granted: sitting down with other restaurant patrons and being served with dignity.

The four men had no idea their actions would reignite the Civil Rights Movement and model a method others would soon follow all across the South. When they sat down at that counter to order coffee, they stood for something far greater: new territory beyond spaces they were currently allowed to occupy. God can use anyone to be a catalyst to spark a movement if they simply believe Him.

Old Testament heroes Caleb and Joshua also believed God for new territory. Caleb said, "We should go up and take possession of the land, for we can certainly do it" (Numbers 13:30). But their fellow Israelites saw themselves in comparison to tribes already in possession of the land and said, "The land we explored devours those living in it" (v. 32). While these other Israelites spied out and sized up their strength and stature in comparison to others, Joshua and Caleb experienced victory through trust in God empowering them. We, too, can trust and enter into God's promises.

> What is standing in front of you that God has given you the ability to possess?

Lord, give me eyes to see and a heart empowered to embrace Your good will for my life.

Numbers 13:26–33; 14:6–9

²⁶ They came back to Moses and Aaron and the whole Israelite community at Kadesh in the Desert of Paran. There they reported to them and to the whole assembly and showed them the fruit of the land. ²⁷ They

gave Moses this account: "We went into the land to which you sent us, and it does flow with milk and honey! Here is its fruit. ²⁸But the people who live there are powerful, and the cities are fortified and very large. We even saw descendants of Anak there. ²⁹The Amalekites live in the Negev; the Hittites, Jebusites and Amorites live in the hill country; and the Canaanites live near the sea and along the Jordan."

³⁰Then Caleb silenced the people before Moses and said, "We should go up and take possession of the land, for we can certainly do it."

³¹But the men who had gone up with him said, "We can't attack those people; they are stronger than we are." ³²And they spread among the Israelites a bad report about the land they had explored. They said, "The land we explored devours those living in it. All the people we saw there are of great size. ³³We saw the Nephilim there (the descendants of Anak come from the Nephilim). We seemed like grasshoppers in our own eyes, and we looked the same to them."

⁶Joshua son of Nun and Caleb son of Jephunneh, who were among those who had explored the land, tore their clothes

[7]and said to the entire Israelite assembly, "The land we passed through and explored is exceedingly good. [8]If the LORD is pleased with us, he will lead us into that land, a land flowing with milk and honey, and will give it to us. [9]Only do not rebel against the LORD. And do not be afraid of the people of the land, because we will devour them. Their protection is gone, but the LORD is with us. Do not be afraid of them."

HANDS AND FEET

Stacy Hawkins Adams

*Share with the Lord's people
who are in need.*

Romans 12:13

Whenever my "spiritual mom" Muriel Miller Branch shares how a chiding from God led her to serve women, I'm reminded that He uses willing vessels like Muriel, a retired middle school librarian and author. Muriel was strolling through a convenience store one day and heard a young mother yelling at her toddler. Muriel muttered, "Someone needs to teach her to do better." As quickly as that declaration filled her spirit, so did God's response: *Why not you?*

Muriel reacted by inviting her personal and professional women friends (including me) to help. We joined her in mentoring younger ladies, sharing advice on parenting, finances, relationships, and more. Muriel named that ministry Women Inspired to Transform (WIT), and for about a decade, we walked alongside her and the dozens she nurtured to wholeness. Her care was similar to the care rendered by the biblical character Dorcas, also known as Tabitha, who was so beloved for her selfless giving that her townspeople successfully pleaded with God's servant to restore her to life (Acts 9:36–42).

The women in Muriel's care experienced restoration because of her consistent love, becoming more attentive mothers, reacclimating after prison, learning to set boundaries, and growing closer to God. "Ma Muriel," as she became known, reminded us through her obedience that, when we know better, we must pay that wisdom forward. God's presence can be deeply felt when we become hands and feet that reflect His loving heart.

> God wants us not simply to react to others' needs as much as He wants Christian believers to act toward others in alignment with His Spirit.

God, use me to show Your love to those around me. When encountering others, God, help me to see their needs and be ready to graciously serve them.

Romans 12:1–16 NLT

¹And so, dear brothers and sisters, I plead with you to give your bodies to God because of all he has done for you. Let them be a living and holy sacrifice—the

kind he will find acceptable. This is truly the way to worship him. ²Don't copy the behavior and customs of this world, but let God transform you into a new person by changing the way you think. Then you will learn to know God's will for you, which is good and pleasing and perfect.

³Because of the privilege and authority God has given me, I give each of you this warning: Don't think you are better than you really are. Be honest in your evaluation of yourselves, measuring yourselves by the faith God has given us. ⁴Just as our bodies have many parts and each part has a special function, ⁵so it is with Christ's body. We are many parts of one body, and we all belong to each other.

⁶In his grace, God has given us different gifts for doing certain things well. So if God has given you the ability to prophesy, speak out with as much faith as God has given you. ⁷If your gift is serving others, serve them well. If you are a teacher, teach well. ⁸If your gift is to encourage others, be encouraging. If it is giving, give generously. If God has given you leadership ability, take the responsibility seriously. And if you have a gift for showing kindness to others, do it gladly.

TELL THE STORY

⁹Don't just pretend to love others. Really love them. Hate what is wrong. Hold tightly to what is good. ¹⁰Love each other with genuine affection, and take delight in honoring each other. ¹¹Never be lazy, but work hard and serve the Lord enthusiastically. ¹²Rejoice in our confident hope. Be patient in trouble, and keep on praying. ¹³When God's people are in need, be ready to help them. Always be eager to practice hospitality.

¹⁴Bless those who persecute you. Don't curse them; pray that God will bless them. ¹⁵Be happy with those who are happy, and weep with those who weep. ¹⁶Live in harmony with each other. Don't be too proud to enjoy the company of ordinary people. And don't think you know it all!

HEAD AND HEART

Tondra L. Loder-Jackson

*He will not shout or cry out, or
raise his voice in the streets.*

Isaiah 42:2

As Dr. Martin Luther King Jr. lay in New York City's Harlem Hospital in 1958, convalescing from a near-fatal stab wound by a deranged woman at a book signing, Christian pastor, theologian, and contemplative Dr. Howard Thurman urged him to ask his doctors to extend his recovery by two weeks. According to Thurman's autobiography, *With Head and Heart,* he counseled King "to reassess himself in relation to the cause, to rest his body and mind with healing detachment, and to take a long look that only solitary brooding can provide."

Thurman has been called the "overlooked civil rights hero" because he preferred transforming society through meditating, preaching, writing, mentoring, and reconciling the races rather than protesting in the streets. He unassumingly counseled several civil rights activists who surpassed his renown: Dr. King, Vernon Jordan, James Farmer, and Reverend Jesse Jackson Sr., to name a few. Akin to Isaiah's prophecy of the coming Messiah, Thurman did "not shout . . . or raise his voice in the streets" (Isaiah 42:2). Rather he helped "[establish] justice on earth" primed through spiritual disciplines that drew him closer to God (v. 4). Isaiah suggests this as a spiritual antidote to human tendencies to falter or be discouraged (v. 4).

A timeless message for today's generation of Christ-led activists: Bringing forth God's justice on earth hinges on an equilibrium between drawing "nearer, my God, to Thee" and saying, "Here am I. Send me!" (6:8).

> In what ways do you maintain your equilibrium as you face life challenges and pursue your purpose?

God, we thank You for the timelessness of Your wisdom and ways.

Isaiah 42:1–4

> [1] Here is my servant, whom I
>   uphold,
>   my chosen one in whom I
>   delight;
> I will put my Spirit on him,

and he will bring justice to
the nations.
²He will not shout or cry out,
or raise his voice in the
streets.
³A bruised reed he will not
break,
and a smoldering wick he
will not snuff out.
In faithfulness he will bring
forth justice;
⁴he will not falter or be
discouraged
till he establishes justice on
earth.
In his teaching the islands
will put their hope.

SIMPLE WISDOM

Melanie Johnson

*But godliness with contentment
is great gain.*
1 Timothy 6:6

The image of an elderly Black woman with a solid grasp on her Bible graces the cover of Oseola McCarty's book *Simple Wisdom for Rich Living* and is memorialized in the bronze monument on the campus of the University of Southern Mississippi (USM). No other image could better depict the source of Ms. McCarty's fulfillment.

Needing to leave school in the sixth grade to work full time in the family laundry business after her aunt's illness, McCarty gained satisfaction in her work of nearly eighty years through her contentment in God. Beginning each day with the Lord's Prayer, she worked from 7:00 in the morning, washing and ironing sometimes well into the night. In rare moments of discouragement, she recited Psalm 23. McCarty wrote in her book: "I find that my life and work are increasing all the time. I am blessed beyond what I hoped."

Before her death, the laundress donated $150,000

of her $280,000 life savings to USM, inspiring a chain of hundreds of thousands of dollars donated to aid students in the scholastic education that life had denied her. She revealed, "My secret was contentment; I was happy with what I had." The rich and simple life of Oseola McCarty leaves us the example that "godliness with contentment is great gain" (1 Timothy 6:6). We, too, can enjoy a rich and rewarding life.

Do you have a solid grasp of the Bible?

God, guide me with Your Word each day
to find satisfaction in my everyday tasks,
and to fulfill Your purposes for me.

Hebrews 13:5–8

⁵Keep your lives free from the love of money and be content with what you have, because God has said,

"Never will I leave you;
never will I forsake you."

⁶So we say with confidence,

"The Lord is my helper; I will
not be afraid.

What can mere mortals do
to me?"

⁷Remember your leaders, who spoke the word of God to you. Consider the outcome of their way of life and imitate their faith. ⁸Jesus Christ is the same yesterday and today and forever.

TAKE ANOTHER LOOK AT JESUS!

Arthur Jackson

But Christ, as the Son, is in charge of God's entire house. And we are God's house, if we keep our courage and remain confident in our hope in Christ.

Hebrews 3:6 NLT

If there ever was a faithful person, it was Brother Justice. He was committed to his marriage, dedicated to his job as a postal worker, and stationed each Sunday at his post as a leader in our local church. When I visited my childhood church not that long ago, perched on the upright piano was the same bell that Brother Justice rang to notify us that the time for weekly instruction was about to end. The bell had endured the test of time. And although Brother Justice has been with the Lord for years, his legacy of faithfulness also endures.

Hebrews 3 brings a faithful servant and a faithful Son to the readers' attention. Though the faithfulness of Moses as God's "servant" is undeniable, it is Jesus whom believers are taught to focus on. "So, dear brothers and sisters . . . think carefully about this Jesus" (v. 1 NLT). Such was the encouragement to those who were being tempted (2:18). Their legacy of faithfulness could come only from following Jesus, the faithful One.

What do we do when the winds of temptation are swirling all around us? When we are weary and worn and want to quit? The text invites us to, as *The Message* renders it, "Take a good hard look at Jesus" (3:1). Look at Him again—and again and again. As we reexamine Jesus, we find the trustworthy Son of God who gives us courage to live in His family.

God wants us to consider Him carefully.

Lord, help me to simply be faithful to You each day.

Hebrews 3:1–6 NLT

¹And so, dear brothers and sisters who belong to God and are partners with those called to heaven, think carefully about this Jesus whom we declare to be God's messenger and High Priest. ²For he was faithful to God, who appointed him, just as Moses served faithfully when he was entrusted with God's entire house.

³But Jesus deserves far more glory than Moses, just as a person who builds a house deserves more praise than the house itself. ⁴For every house has a builder, but the one who built everything is God.

⁵Moses was certainly faithful in God's house as a servant. His work was an illustration of the truths God would reveal later. ⁶But Christ, as the Son, is in charge of God's entire house. And we are God's house, if we keep our courage and remain confident in our hope in Christ.

KEEP RUNNING FOR JESUS

Ekemini Uwan

Therefore, since we are surrounded by such a great cloud of witnesses, let us throw off everything that hinders and the sin that so easily entangles. And let us run with perseverance the race marked out for us.

Hebrews 12:1

I love Black History Month. It provides the opportunity to learn about Black historical figures and Black people in the present walking in their God-given callings and making significant contributions to the Black community and the world. Often when we think of Black History Month, famous civil rights leaders are top of mind because of the rich legacy they left, a legacy we all still benefit from today. But many icons remain in the shadows.

Nannie Helen Burroughs, born in 1878, is one of my heroes. Educator, civil rights pioneer, and public intellectual, she dedicated her life to carving out space for Black women and girls in places where they were excluded, and was a prominent member of several Black women's organizations dedicated to women's rights and racial uplift. One crowning achievement was her founding of the National Training School for Women and Girls in Washington, DC, in 1909, where she was principal for twenty years. She began with nineteen students and built to more than one hundred by 1929.

The school accepted mostly working-class students from the United States, Canada, Africa, Central America, and the West Indies. Nannie loved people and had a deep devotion to our Lord and Savior Jesus Christ, always proclaiming His excellence. She spoke about her life and the school, "It's His work. I began it for Him; I take it to Him day by day."

She saw herself as a servant of the Lord: "God's school on the hill. Who owns the school? Well, one thing is certain. I don't own it . . . what would I do with houses and land? I've put my whole life in this hill, but I have done it for God. He has chosen my little life to build something for humanity, a place where the women and girls of my race can come and learn some sense, about how to live to the glory of God."

Nannie Helen Burroughs and many of our other Black foremothers and forefathers in the faith are part of the "great cloud of witnesses," who encourage us: "Therefore, since we are surrounded by such a great cloud of witnesses, let us throw off everything that hinders and the sin that so easily entangles. And let us run with perseverance the race marked out for us, fixing our eyes on Jesus, the pioneer and perfecter of faith. For the joy set before him he endured the cross, scorning its shame, and sat down at the right hand of the throne of God. Consider him who endured such opposition from sinners, so that you will not grow weary and lose heart" (Hebrews 12:1–3).

Nannie and others fought oppression, discrimination, and countless trials we know nothing about. They persevered by keeping the main thing, the main thing: undivided faith in Jesus Christ. Many did not see the justice and equality they dedicated their life's work to—and truth be told, we are yet fighting for much of the same, as the baton has been passed to us. When prolonged suffering occurs, particularly when it manifests in the form of racial oppression, there is a temptation to take justice into our own hands and, in extreme cases, to renounce the faith and walk away from Jesus altogether. On this side of glory, and from our vantage point, justice comes slowly.

As a kid growing up in my neighborhood, I remember racing the neighborhood kids to see who was the fastest on our block. I immediately got in position, and right when I heard, "On your marks, get set, go!" I took off like a speed racer. Just as I was leaving the competition in the dust, one shoelace got entangled with my other foot and sent me diving to the pavement. In my excitement about the race, I hadn't taken time to tie my shoelaces. I went into the race haphazardly, void of the intentionality necessary to ensure that I could run my race to the very end.

Lessons from Scripture instruct and help us mature. The Holy Spirit, speaking through the writer of Hebrews, knew there would be times when the sinful pleasures of the world would entice and lure us away from the narrow road that leads to life (Matthew 7:14). God exhorts us to throw off everything that hinders us and the sin that entangles us so we can run the race God marked out for each of us. And God gave us Jesus as our example.

Throughout Jesus's life on earth, He was intentional about where He went, when He withdrew to pray, whom He visited and healed, when He ate, when He fasted, and even where He performed miracles. When the time came for Him to suffer on the cross and die for the sins of the world, He did it for the joy set before Him. The joy of knowing He would be reunited with God the Father and seated at His right hand. He did it because He loves us and has gone to prepare a place for us (John 14:3) where we will dwell with the Father, Son, and Holy Spirit in glory (Revelation 21–22).

What hinders and entangles us and keeps us from running our race? Our "race tracks" might look different; they may be paved with suffering, but ultimately the finish line is the same: eternal life together with our God in glory. So let us run with intention as Nannie Helen Burroughs did, and as those numbered among our great cloud of witnesses, fixing our eyes on Jesus, who is the joy set before us.

FAITH IN THE STRUGGLE

Marvin A. McMickle

*The Lord . . . will rescue me from
the hand of this Philistine.*

1 Samuel 17:37

David's encounter with Goliath is an important reference for the life of Martin Luther King Jr. The measure of David's and King's life isn't that they prevailed in the great struggles they confronted. Of greater importance is that each had the courage to enter into struggles no one else thought they could possibly win.

David defeated the giant Philistine warrior, but the fact that David had the faith to face Goliath in the first place is most striking. King Saul wouldn't fight that battle. Nor would any of his soldiers. Even David's brothers trembled at the thunder of Goliath's voice. Armed only with rocks and a slingshot, David went out to face grave danger. The fact that he won against Goliath is secondary to the fact that he went with the faith that he could possibly win.

This is the way to think about Martin Luther King Jr. The issue is not that his efforts helped change the social and political landscape of the United States and many other nations around the world. In the face of laws that supported racial segregation, and in the face of stiff resistance from those determined to maintain that status quo, Dr. King had the courage to take on those gigantic forms of injustice. In the same way we honor David, we should honor Dr. King: not because he won, but because he went out to face a giant foe with no guarantee of winning.

> Do we have the faith of David and Dr. King, that God will sustain us even against our giant foes?

God, the obstacles I face may seem to be too large for me to overcome. Give me faith and courage to face whatever problems and perils may come my way, knowing You will always be with me. Amen.

1 Samuel 17:34–37

34But David said to Saul, "Your servant has been keeping his father's sheep. When a lion or a bear came and carried off a sheep from the flock, 35I went after it, struck it and rescued the sheep from its mouth. When it turned on me, I seized it by its hair, struck it and killed it. [36] Your servant has killed both the lion and the bear; this uncircumcised Philistine will be like one of them, because he has defied the armies of the living God. [37] The LORD who rescued me from the paw of the lion and the paw of the bear will rescue me from the hand of this Philistine."

Saul said to David, "Go, and the LORD be with you."

TELL THE STORY

DEEP ROOTS

Georgia Hill

There is hope for a tree.

Job 14:7

The famous old oak has heavy limbs stretching out like mighty arms. In 1861, abolitionists hired Mary Smith Peake to secretly teach runaway slaves in its shade, defying laws against educating Blacks. She brought lessons of freedom and Christ to whoever wanted to learn, living out her faith gained as a young girl memorizing Scripture. When illness weakened her, this missionary's classroom moved inside her home. When Mary died, the hope of freedom lived. A school was erected by the great oak and, in 1868, Hampton Normal and Agricultural Institute began there. Hope inspired a seed-of-faith classroom that grew into what is now internationally renowned Hampton University.

There's hope for those whose roots grow deep in God. Job experienced this hope amid days "full of trouble" (Job 14:1). Despite the loss of his children, home, and health; failed friendships; and his wife's betrayal, God blessed Job. God also gave hope and freedom to Black people experiencing cruel bondage. God allowed many to fulfill dreams of educated minds and fruitful lives.

How fitting that freedom's words—the first Southern reading of the Emancipation Proclamation—were uttered in 1863 under that Hampton oak where Mary had taught. Neither the poison of slavery nor racism's bitter hatred could dry up the roots of hope in God, who loosens shackles from body, mind, and soul. The Emancipation Oak still stands on the campus of Hampton University, and hope still grows.

What are you hoping for yourself?

Lord, show me how to share Your hope with others.

Job 14:1–9

> [1]Mortals, born of woman,
> are of few days and full of
> trouble.
> [2]They spring up like flowers and
> wither away;
> like fleeting shadows, they
> do not endure.
> [3]Do you fix your eye on them?
> Will you bring them before
> you for judgment?

⁴Who can bring what is pure
      from the impure?
   No one!
⁵A person's days are determined;
      you have decreed the num-
      ber of his months
   and have set limits he can-
      not exceed.
⁶So look away from him and let
      him alone,
   till he has put in his time
      like a hired laborer.

⁷At least there is hope for a tree:
   If it is cut down, it will
      sprout again,
   and its new shoots will not
      fail.
⁸Its roots may grow old in the
      ground
   and its stump die in the soil,
⁹yet at the scent of water it will
      bud
   and put forth shoots like a
      plant.

GIVING UP

Nia Caldwell

*Each of you should give what you
have decided in your heart to give,
not reluctantly or under compulsion,
for God loves a cheerful giver.*

2 Corinthians 9:7

The late Kobe Bryant is considered one of the greatest basketball players ever. In his drive to become the best, he reportedly slept only about four hours each night. He said, "There's a choice that we have to make as people, as individuals. If you want to be great at something . . . there are sacrifices that come along with that."

Sacrifice not only helps us to accomplish our major life and career goals but also contributes to our hopes of pleasing God.

When God asked Abraham to sacrifice his son, instead of questioning Him, Abraham prepared to do as God called him to do, by faith. As he was about to slay his son, an angel of God stopped him and said, "Do not lay a hand on the boy. . . . Do not do anything to him. Now I know that you fear God, because you have not withheld from me your son"

(Genesis 22:12). Abraham honored God's command to sacrifice what he had waited so many decades to receive, the son Sarah had borne, the child of the promise Abraham cared so much about. God saw Abraham's heart of faith and blessed him.

Although God asked Abraham to sacrifice something he treasured, God didn't leave him hanging. God provided a ram to sacrifice in the place of Isaac. We can be comforted by the fact that God always has our backs. Anything that we sacrifice for *His* will can be restored and is small in comparison to what God has provided for us.

> What sacrifices are you making
> right now in order to obey God?

Dear God, I don't want to miss out on what You have planned for me due to my inability to give things up. Open my heart to give what You call me to so that I can live according to Your truth.

Genesis 22:1–18

¹Some time later God tested Abraham. He said to him, "Abraham!"

"Here I am," he replied.

²Then God said, "Take your son, your only son, whom you love—Isaac—and go to the region of Moriah. Sacrifice him there as

a burnt offering on a mountain I will show you."

³Early the next morning Abraham got up and loaded his donkey. He took with him two of his servants and his son Isaac. When he had cut enough wood for the burnt offering, he set out for the place God had told him about. ⁴On the third day Abraham looked up and saw the place in the distance. ⁵He said to his servants, "Stay here with the donkey while I and the boy go over there. We will worship and then we will come back to you."

⁶Abraham took the wood for the burnt offering and placed it on his son Isaac, and he himself carried the fire and the knife. As the two of them went on together, ⁷Isaac spoke up and said to his father Abraham, "Father?"

"Yes, my son?" Abraham replied.

"The fire and wood are here," Isaac said, "but where is the lamb for the burnt offering?"

⁸Abraham answered, "God himself will provide the lamb for the burnt offering, my son." And the two of them went on together.

⁹When they reached the place God had told him about, Abraham built an altar there and arranged the wood on it. He bound his son Isaac and laid him on the altar, on top of the wood. ¹⁰Then he reached out his hand

TELL THE STORY

and took the knife to slay his son. [11]But the angel of the LORD called out to him from heaven, "Abraham! Abraham!"

"Here I am," he replied.

[12]"Do not lay a hand on the boy," he said. "Do not do anything to him. Now I know that you fear God, because you have not withheld from me your son, your only son."

[13]Abraham looked up and there in a thicket he saw a ram caught by its horns. He went over and took the ram and sacrificed it as a burnt offering instead of his son. [14]So Abraham called that place The LORD Will Provide. And to this day it is said, "On the mountain of the LORD it will be provided."

[15]The angel of the LORD called to Abraham from heaven a second time [16]and said, "I swear by myself, declares the LORD, that because you have done this and have not withheld your son, your only son, [17]I will surely bless you and make your descendants as numerous as the stars in the sky and as the sand on the seashore. Your descendants will take possession of the cities of their enemies, [18]and through your offspring all nations on earth will be blessed, because you have obeyed me."

HUMILITY TO THE RESCUE

Cherie Trahan

Have the same mindset as Christ Jesus.

Philippians 2:5

In 1849, Harriet Tubman made her daring escape from slavery. She, however, gave in to her compassion toward family and friends who remained in bondage. Harriet sacrificed her taste of freedom's glory to travel back and forth between the oppressive fields of Maryland and the liberating plains of Philadelphia. She made thirteen subsequent missions, using the Underground Railroad network, and rescued about seventy other souls with humble ambition.

Further defining her extraordinary success were Harriet's well-documented visions and vivid dreams. Recorded by fellow abolitionists, writers, and her own words, Harriet believed her visions and dreams were God-sent revelations that did help guide her and the others she led safely. I'd learned about this big part of her life and her passionate faith in God, and I could see myself in her. I gained strengthened reassurance about God's direct messages to me through vivid night dreams and their divine manifestations in my life, as I humbly journaled about them often.

Paul illustrates humility for us in Philippians 2 with Jesus being our supreme example. The Savior of the world gave up His divine privileges and sacrificed His life on the cross to rescue humanity from sin. With a similar heart, once we arrive on the other side of salvation through Christ Jesus, we should resist delighting in this alone. Equipped with compassion and our own experiences with God's relational nature, we can help lead other souls to eternal freedom through our confident witness and humble discipleship.

> Jesus is our best example of humility.

Father, help me to be more humble,
as I consider Jesus's example.

Philippians 2:1–8

> [1] Therefore if you have any encouragement
> from being united with Christ, if any
> comfort from his love, if any common
> sharing in the Spirit, if any tenderness and
> compassion, [2] then make my joy complete
> by being like-minded, having the same

love, being one in spirit and of one mind.
³Do nothing out of selfish ambition or vain
conceit. Rather, in humility value others
above yourselves, ⁴not looking to your own
interests but each of you to the interests of
the others.

⁵In your relationships with one another,
have the same mindset as Christ Jesus:

> ⁶Who, being in very nature
>   God,
>   did not consider equal-
>   ity with God something
>   to be used to his own
>   advantage;
> ⁷rather, he made himself
>   nothing
>   by taking the very nature of
>   a servant,
>   being made in human
>   likeness.
> ⁸And being found in appearance
>   as a man,
>   he humbled himself
>   by becoming obedient to
>   death—
>   even death on a cross!

THANK YOU, LORD!

Michelle R. Loyd-Paige

*Sing psalms and hymns and spiritual
songs to God with thankful hearts.*

Colossians 3:16 NLT

Every time I hear Mahalia Jackson sing the lyrics
of gospel artist Thomas Dorsey's "Precious Lord,
take my hand," I'm reminded that whatever challenge I'm facing, it's not new to human experience
and God will see me through—as He has for generations of African Americans and other Christian
believers before me.

There's nothing like hearing a Spirit-filled gospel
message or an uplifting gospel song to refocus one's
thoughts toward God's faithfulness on those days
when life seems particularly challenging. The unfolding of African American history is an ongoing
story of challenging days—slavery, Jim Crow, and
seemingly never-ending days of discrimination.
However, amid these challenges, one also finds the
sounds of gratitude, joy, and hope. Those sounds
are the loudest and strongest on Sunday morning.

On Sunday morning, sermons that acknowledge
our hardships, yet give God glory, encourage those

gathered to keep the faith. This is something pioneering African American preachers and church-builders like Bishop Richard Allen, preacher and author Jarena Lee, and more knew quite well. On Sunday morning, songs like "We've Come This Far by Faith" by Albert Goodson, and "The Lord Will Make a Way Somehow," also written by Dorsey, are a reminder of God's faithfulness.

Through the preached Word we grow in the deep knowledge and assurance that, despite our struggles, God is with us and loves us. Singing "to God with thankful hearts" (Colossians 3:16 NLT) strengthens us in the midst of trials.

> Humming and singing alone and with others can inspire our memories of God and buoy our spirit.

Thank You, Lord, for the stories of Your faithfulness expressed in worship songs and for the gifted voices that ingrain them on my heart.

Colossians 3:15–17 NLT

[15] And let the peace that comes from Christ rule in your hearts. For as members of one body you are called to live in peace. And always be thankful.

[16]Let the message about Christ, in all its richness, fill your lives. Teach and counsel each other with all the wisdom he gives. Sing psalms and hymns and spiritual songs to God with thankful hearts. [17]And whatever you do or say, do it as a representative of the Lord Jesus, giving thanks through him to God the Father.

BAPTIZED INTO CHRIST

Marvin Williams

Don't you know that all of us who were baptized into Christ Jesus were baptized into his death? We were therefore buried with him through baptism into death in order that, just as Christ was raised from the dead through the glory of the Father, we too may live a new life.

Romans 6:3–4

On the morning of November 1, 1977, after Pastor Davidson preached, he "opened the doors of the church." The deacons put chairs in the front of the sanctuary. After a long tussle with God and tears streaming down my face, I made that slow walk to the front of the sanctuary and sat in a chair. Pastor Davidson asked me why I came up, and I whispered to him and the waiting congregation that I wanted to be a child of God. I didn't know what that meant, as I had never used the phrase before. Now I know that it was the Spirit who gave me those words and the desire to be transformed by the gospel. That morning, a thirteen-year-old Black boy from the West Side of Chicago placed his faith in Christ.

Later that evening, Pastor Davidson and I stood in the middle of the old baptistry, and he uttered those famous words: "In obedience to the great Head of the Church and upon the profession of your faith, young man, I baptize you in the name of the Father, and of the Son, and of the Holy Spirit." Then, he buried me in the "watery grave" and brought me back up out of the water. My old life as a thief, a liar, and a disobedient son died and was buried with Christ through immersion in the water, and I was raised to new life with Christ through emergence from the water. I felt new. My baptism was one of the most powerful and iconic moments in my journey with Jesus. But what was a feeling of joy, freedom, and hope for me would have been a continued nightmare of bondage and hopelessness for slaves in Virginia in 1667.

On September 23, 1667, the beautiful icon of baptism was sullied by an evil and infamous decision. Slave owners feared that slaves would recognize their faith in Christ and subsequent baptism would reveal to them their equality to their supposed superiors. Owners feared undermining the justification of their subjugation and breaking the chains of spiritual, psychological, and physical slavery. In a break from centuries of precedent in

Europe, the Virginia Assembly passed a law that said Christian baptism would not free enslaved persons in the colonies: "It is enacted and declared by this grand assembly, and the authority thereof, that the conferring of baptisme doth not alter the condition of their person as to his bondage or freedom." This law was a mockery to the powerful significance, symbolism, and hope of Christian baptism that Paul highlighted in Romans 6.

At the beginning of chapter 6, Paul explained to the Christians in Rome that it was illogical for them to continue sinning in order to give grace a chance to operate. To emphatically illustrate what it meant to die to sin and live a new life in Christ, Paul turned to baptism (vv. 3–4), the rite of initiation into the kingdom of God and into the life of the church with God's people. For Paul, being baptized was not just some comforting ritual. It was closely connected with the genuine confession of faith in Christ that preceded it. Moreover, this confession of faith and subsequent baptism evoked images of a radical transformation of the person and their relationship to the social order. Individuals came to a decision to follow Christ. That meant they would tear their lives up from the roots and orient their lives around a new set of kingdom values and habits. This meant nothing short of starting their lives over again in close relationship with Christ. Paul illustrated this point when he urged

Philemon to free Onesimus as a sign of their fellowship in Christ (Philemon 1:12–19). Thus, the Christian initiation of baptism meant being identified and united with Christ in His death and dying to an entire way of life—daily. The Christian who understood the symbolism and significance of this aspect of baptism was free from the power of his old way of living and could not easily go back to the former life.

Not only were these new believers baptized into Christ's death, but they were also buried with Him through that same baptism. Baptism symbolized not only that their old way of life had died but that it was also buried with Christ (Romans 6:4), highlighting the finality of the death to sin. But their baptism into Jesus's death and burial was not the end of the story. There was more. There was hope for something different. Hope for something better. Christ's death and burial were followed by resurrection. So, too, the believers' death and burial to their old way of life were followed by being raised to the hope and freedom to live a new life (v. 4). Believing the gospel and being baptized were not supposed to lead to continued bondage (especially bondage to professed Christians); it was to be viewed and experienced as a powerful symbol of being united to the Son, who sets us free indeed (John 8:36). It's also a symbol of the new life we have with the family of God that ought to be characterized by freedom.

Sin has a way of being an evil dictator, controlling and dominating our lives. It manifests itself in dysfunction, self-centeredness, systems of racial injustice, and even racializing something as beautiful and powerful as Christian baptism, as the Virginia slave law did. But Christ, who is the source of truth, exercises His full authority to liberate us from the tyranny of personal and systemic sin and to offer us hope of new life in Him. Like putting on a new coat, Christian baptism is still one of the most powerful symbols of being clothed with Christ (Galatians 3:27) with all the benefits of joy, freedom, and hope.

SERVING IN SACRIFICE

Patricia Raybon

*And do not forget to do good
and to share with others, for with
such sacrifices God is pleased.*

Hebrews 13:16

The Nashville man needed a doctor, but didn't have health insurance. God provided help, however, at one of the historically Black colleges and universities, an HBCU. Meharry Medical College's free Saltwagon Clinic is a student-run treatment center supervised by faculty physicians serving with medical students as volunteers. "People like myself who don't have insurance right now can come here and get real good medical help," the man said. "Also, my joy is I'm helping the future doctors of this community, so that Nashville is better and the doctors are good at what they do."

As one Meharry student explained, "The most rewarding thing about volunteering at the clinic is [knowing] I'm making a difference." He explained, "Despite living in America, one of the most privileged nations in the world, there are still people out there who don't have health insurance and who are in need of these kind of services."

Sacrificing our time and skills to help those who need it most embodies Jesus's declaration that "it is more blessed to give than to receive" (Acts 20:35). That ethic reflects Meharry's long-held mission to serve minority and underserved communities by training doctors who'll provide high-quality "health *caring*." In that way, Meharry's graduates commit to help end health disparities. It's a godly mission. As the writer of Hebrews exhorted, "Do not forget to do good and to share with others, for with such sacrifices God is pleased" (13:16).

Caring for others is *doing* good.

God, thank You for the care You show to me through others. Help me to be Your servant and to do good to others in my family and community, and to those outside my community who need help.

Acts 20:32–35

³²Now I commit you to God and to the word of his grace, which can build you up and give you an inheritance among all those who are sanctified. ³³I have not coveted anyone's silver or gold or clothing. ³⁴You

yourselves know that these hands of mine have supplied my own needs and the needs of my companions.[35] In everything I did, I showed you that by this kind of hard work we must help the weak, remembering the words the Lord Jesus himself said: "It is more blessed to give than to receive."

THE LIVING PAST

Carey H. Latimore IV

*Remember the days of old; consider
the generations long past. Ask your
father and he will tell you, your
elders, and they will explain to you.*

Deuteronomy 32:7

"Work songs" and Negro spirituals were a passion for musical prodigy R. Nathaniel Dett. Dett's family and church encouraged him to appreciate varied works from diverse poets and composers, especially songs his ancestors had sung while enslaved. Though others abandoned this music hearkening back to a painful past, Dett preserved the songs as crucial to Black heritage and self-esteem.

After his studies at Oberlin Conservatory of Music, Dett served as director of music at Hampton Institute (Hampton University) from 1913 to 1933. He introduced his students to the spirituals and work songs he loved, so Hampton's choirs could share their beauty and value with people from all backgrounds. As the choirs traveled the world, they carried with them this legacy, memorializing traditional Black music.

God instructed Joshua in how to memorialize the nation of Israel's crossing of the Jordan River, a pivotal moment in their journey from slavery. Commanding Joshua to appoint one man from each of the twelve tribes to carry a stone from the river, God caused these stones to become physical memorials for future generations to see God's power (Joshua 4:2–7).

God wants us to understand the past and His role across cultures and in our individual lives. Indeed, God's omnipotence throughout history is alive in our stories. We can continue to remember the ways our past illuminates God's transcendence and provision for all. We can be living stones.

We can study to better understand
and share our history and
God's plan with others.

Lord, thank You for the desire, opportunities, and methods You give me to be a witness of Your faithfulness.

Joshua 4:1–7

¹When the whole nation had finished crossing the Jordan, the LORD said to Joshua, ²"Choose twelve men from among the people, one from each tribe, ³and tell them to take up twelve stones from the

middle of the Jordan, from right where the priests are standing, and carry them over with you and put them down at the place where you stay tonight."

⁴So Joshua called together the twelve men he had appointed from the Israelites, one from each tribe, ⁵and said to them, "Go over before the ark of the LORD your God into the middle of the Jordan. Each of you is to take up a stone on his shoulder, according to the number of the tribes of the Israelites, ⁶to serve as a sign among you. In the future, when your children ask you, 'What do these stones mean?' ⁷tell them that the flow of the Jordan was cut off before the ark of the covenant of the LORD. When it crossed the Jordan, the waters of the Jordan were cut off. These stones are to be a memorial to the people of Israel forever."

TELL THE STORY

LOVING WITH OUR MINDS

Roslyn Yilpet

Jesus replied: "Love the Lord your God with all your heart and with all your soul and with all your mind."

Matthew 22:37

Though Ida Bell Wells-Barnett was born a slave in cruel conditions, her studies at a Black university her father helped found shaped her mind, heart, and spirit to serve others. That college was Shaw University, known today as Rust College. Wells also studied at Fisk University.

She wrote, "The way to right wrongs is to turn the light of truth on them." Wells turned the light on the lynching of Black people. She became an anti-lynching activist, investigating and exposing these acts of violence, publishing and marching against the evil.

Through Black and Christian audiences, Wells gained support for her writing, lectures, and protests, and pursued anti-lynching laws in meetings with leaders at the White House and in Europe.

She also worked with the National Equal Rights League, and helped found the National Association for the Advancement of Colored People. Wells also established the National Organization of Colored Women, marching also for women's rights, and even planted the first kindergarten in her community. She loved helping others.

Offering ourselves as a "living sacrifice, holy and pleasing to God," addressed by the apostle Paul writing in Romans 12:1, proclaims—publishes—the love of Christ. God's love for us compels love of neighbor in our minds and empowers our hearts to act on others' behalf. Loving God transforms each one of us to understand how to live, and how to love others.

> We can express God's love to our neighbor in many different ways.

Lord, help me to love my neighbor in Your strength and with Your wisdom—not my own.

Romans 12:1–12

¹Therefore, I urge you, brothers and sisters, in view of God's mercy, to offer your bodies as a living sacrifice, holy and pleasing to God—this is your true and proper worship. ²Do not conform to the pattern of this

world, but be transformed by the renewing of your mind. Then you will be able to test and approve what God's will is—his good, pleasing and perfect will.

³For by the grace given me I say to every one of you: Do not think of yourself more highly than you ought, but rather think of yourself with sober judgment, in accordance with the faith God has distributed to each of you. ⁴For just as each of us has one body with many members, and these members do not all have the same function, ⁵so in Christ we, though many, form one body, and each member belongs to all the others. ⁶We have different gifts, according to the grace given to each of us. If your gift is prophesying, then prophesy in accordance with your faith; ⁷if it is serving, then serve; if it is teaching, then teach; ⁸if it is to encourage, then give encouragement; if it is giving, then give generously; if it is to lead, do it diligently; if it is to show mercy, do it cheerfully.

⁹Love must be sincere. Hate what is evil; cling to what is good. ¹⁰Be devoted to one another in love. Honor one another above yourselves. ¹¹Never be lacking in zeal, but keep your spiritual fervor, serving the Lord. ¹²Be joyful in hope, patient in affliction, faithful in prayer.

HOW THE WALLS CAME DOWN

Rasool Berry

Now the gates of Jericho were securely barred because of the Israelites. No one went out and no one came in.

Joshua 6:1

A decorated Marine and World War II veteran, Cecil B. Moore fought against Nazi tyranny. Yet Moore and other Black soldiers were then denied at home the liberation they battled to secure for others. Racism and segregation remained the norm. In 1953, Moore became a civil rights lawyer, and battled an imposing fortress of racial inequality in Philadelphia: Girard College. This lavish college preparatory school founded in 1848 for "White male orphans" boasted a ten-foot wall enclosing its North Philadelphia campus, serving notice to the poor, Black community surrounding it: No Black children welcome!

Moore organized a peaceful protest in 1965. Dr. Martin Luther King Jr. joined Moore's march to desegregate Girard College. Moore's marches continued every day, for seven months and seventeen days until a landmark court decision forced Girard to integrate!

Twenty years after Moore's march, my mother enrolled my brother and me in Girard. The free, quality education we received opened new doors, academically and spiritually. I would later become the first in my family to graduate from college. While attending Girard, I learned that Jesus broke down walls on the cross: between humanity and God, between the oppressed and liberation, and between anything the enemy of our souls would use to divide us.

Jesus is a wall-breaker: "For he himself is our peace, who has made the two groups one and has destroyed the barrier, the dividing wall of hostility" (Ephesians 2:14).

> The same God who empowered Joshua to tear down the walls of Jericho is still breaking down the walls of injustice and division today. What walls have been broken down for you?

God, keep my focus on my faith and trust in You and Your power to break down walls of injustice.

Joshua 6:1–5

¹Now the gates of Jericho were securely barred because of the Israelites. No one went out and no one came in.

²Then the LORD said to Joshua, "See, I have delivered Jericho into your hands, along with its king and its fighting men. ³March around the city once with all the armed men. Do this for six days. ⁴Have seven priests carry trumpets of rams' horns in front of the ark. On the seventh day, march around the city seven times, with the priests blowing the trumpets. ⁵When you hear them sound a long blast on the trumpets, have the whole army give a loud shout; then the wall of the city will collapse and the army will go up, everyone straight in."

TELL THE STORY

A SIGNATURE PIECE

Kimya Loder

You created my inmost being; you knit me together in my mother's womb.

Psalm 139:13

Bursts of blue and red outline the animated images of a jazz quartet grooving to the rhythm and blues. This vibrant illustration decorates a patch in the painted quilt *Jazz Stories* by Faith Ringgold. This artist is known for her unique form of quilting that colorfully tells the story of the culture and traditions of African Americans. One reviewer wrote: "By sewing soft pictures, with narrative imagery and colorful motifs, Faith Ringgold persists in making a strong and memorable impact." *Memorable*, the perfect word to describe the distinctive, signature pieces that reveal the intention and identity of their creator.

If we view our lives as signature pieces, what do they tell the world about the God who created us? God, our Maker, proactively and intentionally crafted each of us before we were introduced to the world (Psalm 139:13). We're "fearfully and won-derfully made" not because of the affirmation we receive from the world or even the standards we impose on ourselves, but because we're designed by a Creator whose "works are wonderful" (v. 14).

We see evidence of God's craftsmanship in everything from the vast oceans to the mountains lining the skies. Our Creator's intentions are re-vealed to us in Scripture where He outlines His purpose for our lives (Ephesians 2:10). May we seek to understand the God who designed us and become more intentional about living in a way that reflects His abundant goodness as He provides what we need.

How can you ensure that your life
reflects God's craftsmanship?

*Thank You, God, for creating me in Your image,
intentionally and purposefully. Help me to
live a life that's a reflection of Your will.*

Psalm 139:13–18

13 For you created my inmost
      being;
   you knit me together in my
      mother's womb.

¹⁴I praise you because I am
fearfully and wonderfully
made;
your works are wonderful,
I know that full well.
¹⁵My frame was not hidden
from you
when I was made in the
secret place,
when I was woven together
in the depths of the earth.
¹⁶Your eyes saw my unformed
body;
all the days ordained for me
were written in your book
before one of them came
to be.
¹⁷How precious to me are your
thoughts, God!
How vast is the sum of
them!
¹⁸Were I to count them,
they would outnumber the
grains of sand—
when I awake, I am still
with you.

ANTHEM OF HOPE

Karynthia Phillips

*But let justice roll on like a river,
righteousness like a never-failing stream!*

Amos 5:24

In song lyrics conceived during turbulent times, the Black Church has voiced messages of strength to persevere. In the struggle against social injustices, voices lifted, chanting through the ups and downs of cultural oppression. Rhythms echoed from Africa to plantation fields to pews of modern churches, responding against persecution. "Lift Every Voice and Sing," a poem by James Weldon Johnson, evolved into the "Black National Anthem" after John Rosamund Johnson, James's brother, added music.

As a college freshman hearing this song during Fisk University chapel, I reflected on my ancestors' struggles. Its verses were also celebratory, with a call to remain vigilant, strategic, and optimistic. The lyrics continue to underscore the hope of progress.

The prophet Amos's words remind us that God's justice is unending, and will rectify all unholy acts while replenishing the earth with compassion and hope (Amos 5).

We need the Spirit to remind us that God alone gives us the strength to do what He requires, to act justly, love mercy, and walk humbly with Him, lifting our voices in advocacy, worship, and service, until ultimate victory is won for all of God's children. Singing the anthem helps to remind us that there is hope with God.

"Lift Every Voice and Sing"

> Lift every voice and sing,
> Till earth and heaven ring,
> Ring with the harmonies of
>   Liberty,
> Let our rejoicing rise
> High as the list'ning skies,
> Let it resound loud as the roll-
>   ing sea.
>
> Sing a song full of the faith that
>   the dark past has taught us
> Sing a song full of the hope that
>   the present has brought us
> Facing the rising sun of our new
>   day begun,
> Let us march on till victory is
>   won.

Stony the road we trod
Bitter the chast'ning rod,
Felt in the days when hope
        unborn had died;
Yet with a steady beat
Have not our weary feet
Come to the place for which
        our fathers sighed?

We have come over a way
        that with tears has been
        watered
We have come, treading our
        path thro' the blood of the
        slaughtered,
Out from the gloomy past, till
        now we stand at last
Where the white gleam of our
        bright star is cast.

God of our weary years,
God of our silent tears,
Thou who hast brought us thus
        far on the way;
Thou who hast by Thy might,
Led us into the light, Keep us
        forever in the path, we
        pray.

TELL THE STORY

Lest our feet stray from the
            places, our God, where we
            meet Thee,

Lest our hearts, drunk with
            the wine of the world we
            forget Thee;
Shadowed beneath Thy hand,
            may we forever stand,
True to our God, true to our
            native land.

> James Rosamund Johnson and
> James Weldon Johnson

PERMISSIONS

OTHER TITLES IN THE VOICES COLLECTION

Available at

https://ourdailybreadpublishing.org/voicescollection.html,
Amazon, or your local bookstore.

VOICES | Our Daily Bread.

Help us get the word out!

Our Daily Bread Publishing exists to feed the soul
with the Word of God.

If you appreciated this book, please let others know.

- Pick up another copy to give as a gift.
- Share a link to the book or mention it
  on social media.
- Write a review on your blog, on a
  bookseller's website, or at our own
  site (odb.org/store).
- Recommend this book for your church,
  book club, or small group.

Connect with us:

 @ourdailybread

 @ourdailybread

 @ourdailybread

Our Daily Bread Publishing
PO Box 3566
Grand Rapids, Michigan 49501 USA

✉ books@odb.org